Welcome

Welcome to the new **ProPoints** ~~nation~~, we're eating out more than ever before. And with such a wide range of cuisines available to us, learning how to manage menus and meals 'on the go' is a crucial part of long term weight loss success. **'Eat Out'** is your indispensable guide to making smart menu choices when you're eating away from home.

The new **ProPoints** plan is our most flexible ever, designed to help you live life as you want and still lose weight. And armed with **'Eat Out'**, you'll be able to stick to the plan wherever you go – enjoying fast food, pub food, restaurant food, and whatever you're doing – shopping, eating a working lunch or enjoying a family day out.

This new 2011 edition has been completely revised and updated with new **ProPoints** values which take into account how the body processes different nutrients in food. It features 68 restaurants and cuisines, from All Bar One to Zizzi, conveniently split into 'cuisine categories' making it easier for you to find the information you need. There's a 'Sandwich' section, information on 'Drinking Out' and lots of helpful information so you can enjoy eating out. Bon Appétit.

About Eat Out *ProPoints* values

The **ProPoints** values listed in this guide are based on menus and nutritional values of featured outlets at the time of publication and are correct at the time of going to print (July 2010). Restaurants may change their menus seasonally, so what's on offer may vary depending on when you visit – but we've tried to include as many dishes as possible that are offered all year round. Also, a restaurant chain's offering may vary by location and this can affect the **ProPoints** values.

The **ProPoints** values listed for the item are 'as served', that is as it is described on the menu, unless otherwise stated. If you have any additional accompaniments, you'll need to add the **ProPoints** values of those too.

For the general category restaurants (e.g. French) the **ProPoints** values have been calculated based on 'average' portions in 'standard' restaurants and should be used as a guide as individual restaurants may vary.

Contents

This guide is split into 'cuisine' categories so it's easy for you to find the information you need. And there's an index on page 154 which lists all the restaurants/cuisines alphabetically.

Please note that although we endeavour to feature as many popular restaurants and outlets as we can, you may notice that some restaurants are not included. This is because they are not able to provide nutritional information at this time, so we cannot calculate the *ProPoints* values of their menus.

Enjoy eating out

Plan ahead – the more you plan, the more in control you'll feel...

- Use your weekly *ProPoints* allowance to give you more flexibility. You could allocate a specific number of *ProPoints* values for your meal out or even spend it all on one occasion if that suits you best.

- Don't arrive too hungry – it could lead you off track. Instead, focus on **Filling & Healthy** foods during the day or have some zero *ProPoints* value soup before you go.

- Have a game plan – if you can choose where to eat, pick somewhere with healthy choices on the menu. Even if it's not your choice, try and find out what they serve and make your menu decisions before you get there.

Take control – make informed choices and enjoy yourself...

- Banish the bread basket – if you don't have the *ProPoints* values to spend on bread (or olives) then ask the waiter not to bring them or at least make sure they aren't put in front of you.

- Soup can be a super choice – generally low in *ProPoints* values, it helps to fill you up. Look for soups that are full of vegetables and aren't cream based.

- Ask and you shall receive – don't be shy about making special requests, staff will be happy to tell you what's in a menu option or to serve dressings and sauces on the side.

- Get yours in first – listening to everyone else's choices can be pretty tempting so place your order first if you can.

- Focus on nice words – like grilled, baked, steamed, poached, roasted (and skip past words like buttery, breaded, fried, creamed, battered).

Troubleshooting – it's never too late to redeem yourself...

- If things don't go to plan, don't worry, don't panic and don't give up. Tomorrow is a new day with a new daily *ProPoints* allowance. And you can always earn activity *ProPoints* values and put them towards your weight loss.

Find out more in your *ProPoints* programme material.

Asian

Some like it hot. In a recent survey, Chinese food was voted the nation's favourite, with Indian food close on their heels. So if you're visiting one of the thousands of Asian restaurants in the UK, here are our top tips…

Chinese

- Avoid deep fried starters and choose a tasty clear soup instead.
- Try chopsticks. They slow down the speed at which you eat – particularly if you're not very good at using them.
- Choose plain boiled rice over egg fried – you can save up to 4 *ProPoints* values.

Indian

- Instead of creamy foods like Kormas and Tikka Masalas, go for vegetable dishes like Rogan Josh or Saag.
- Chicken Tikka, Chicken Shashlick or Tandoori Prawns are great choices – high on taste, lower on *ProPoints* values.
- Plain steamed rice is lower in *ProPoints* values than pilau, and chapati bread is lower than naan.

Thai

- Watch out for dishes made with lots of coconut milk or peanut sauce (Thai Green, Mussaman or Penang curries for example) – they are laden with *ProPoints* values.
- Garlic Fried Prawns (Goong Tod Gratiem Prik Thai) and Sweet & Sour Prawns (Priaw Wahn Goong) are delicious with plain steamed rice and are relatively low in *ProPoints* values.

Japanese (Sushi)

- Limit the extras – mayonnaise, cream cheese and creamy Japanese dressings on the salad can add significant *ProPoints* values to your meal.
- Avoid the feeding frenzy – it's easy to get carried away when taking food off the conveyor belt. Consider your options as you would in any other restaurant.
- Start smart – a low *ProPoints* values starter will help to fill you up and start you off on the right track – try Miso soup or Edamame (baby soy beans in the pod).

Starters

Chicken & Sweetcorn Soup	6
Hot & Sour Soup	4
Prawn Crackers (average portion)	9
Seaweed (Deep Fried)	9
Sesame Prawn Fingers (each)	3
Spring Rolls (each)	9

Main Courses

Aromatic Crispy Duck with Pancakes (per Filled Pancake)	9
Char Sui Pork	11
Chicken & Cashew Nuts	9
Chicken Foo Yung	15
Chicken in Black Bean Sauce	11
Chicken with Mushroom	8
Duck with Chinese Mushroom & Bamboo Shoots	13
Green Pepper Beef in Black Bean Sauce	12
Kung Po Chicken	9
Lemon Chicken	10
Mushroom Chow Mein	6
Mushroom Foo Yung	8
Prawns with Ginger & Vegetables	10
Roast Pork Cantonese Style	10
Special Chow Mein	9
Sweet & Sour Chicken (Balls or Peking style)	13
Sweet & Sour Prawns	10
Szechuan Prawn with Vegetables	12
Vegetable Curry	8

Side Orders

Egg Fried Rice	16
Mixed Chinese Vegetables in Oyster Sauce	6
Plain Boiled Rice	12
Rice Noodles 'Singapore' Style	14
Special Fried Rice	23
Stir-Fried Beansprouts with Garlic & Spring Onion	4
Stir-Fried Vegetables	4

Desserts

Fortune Cookies (each)	2
Ice Cream	9
Lychees (6)	0
Toffee Banana	15

Starters

Chicken Seekh Kebab	9
Chicken Shashlick	9
Chicken Tikka (4 pieces)	6
Dahl Soup	14
Meat Samosa (each)	9
Onion Bhajee (each)	8
Prawn Puri	10
Seekh Kebab	11
Tandoori Chicken Quarter	6
Tandoori King Prawn	6
Tandoori Mixed Grill	11
Vegetable Samosa (each)	7

Main Course – Balti Dishes

Chicken	18
Chicken Korma	24
Chicken Tikka Masala	23
Dahl	15
Fish Curry	18
Lamb	23

Main Course – Chicken Dishes

Biryani	37
Ceylon	30
Dhansak	30
Dopiaza	25
Jalfrezi	24
Kashmir	30
Korma	24
Madras	27
Pasanda	25
Saag	23
Tikka (8 pieces)	14
Tikka Masala	23
Vindaloo	23
Tandoori Chicken (half)	15

Main Course – King Prawn Dishes

Madras	19
Vindaloo	15

Main Course – Lamb Dishes

Biryani	40
Korma	34
Pasanda	34
Rogan Josh	29

Main Course – Prawn Dishes

Biryani	29
Ceylon	23
Chilli Masala	17
Dhansak	23
Dopiaza	17
Jalfrezi	16
Kashmir	22
Korma	22
Madras	19
Pasanda	17
Saag	16
Vindaloo	15

Main Course – Vegetarian Dishes

Vegetable Biryani	29
Vegetable Curry	15

Side Orders

Bombay Potato	8
Cauliflower Bhajee	6
Chapati	12
Cucumber Raita (per teaspoon)	2
Keema Naan	21
Lime Pickle (per teaspoon)	1
Mango Chutney (per teaspoon)	1
Mushroom Bhajee	9
Paratha	10
Peshwari Naan	18
Pilau Rice	16
Plain Basmati Rice	12
Plain Boiled Rice	12
Plain Naan	12
Poppadom	4
Saag Aloo	8
Stuffed Paratha	16

* Please note – the *ProPoints* values for all mains (apart from Biryani dishes) are without rice or other accompaniments.

Starters

Chicken Satay – Sateh Gai	8
Fried Spicy Fish Cake (each) – Tod Man Pla	5
Fried Spring Roll (each) – Popia Tod	4
Fried Won-Ton (each) – Keau-Krob	2
Glass Noodle Soup	8
Hot & Sour Chicken Soup – Tom Yam Gai	7
Mussels with Coriander & Beansprouts – Hoi Tord	5
Prawn Crackers, 30g	4
Prawn Satay – Goong Sateh	8
Red Radish Soup	2
Sweet Chilli Dipping Sauce, 30g	2
Thai Dumpling (each) – Ka-Nom-Jeeb	1
Thai Noodle Soup – Gange Chud Woon Sen	8
Watercress & Beansprouts	0

Main Courses

BBQ Pork Spareribs – Sikrong Mu Ping	22
Beef, Chicken or Pork Green Curry – Gaeng Keo Wan	20
Beef, Chicken or Pork Red Curry – Gaeng Phed	23
Beef with Oyster Sauce – Neau Pad Namman Hoi	14
Chicken with Cashews – Gai Pad Med Ma-Muang	15
Chicken with Mushrooms – Gai Pad Hed Sod	12
Duck with Tamarind & Honey – Ped Makham	20
Garlic Fried Prawns – Goong Tod Gratiem Prik Thai	9
Steamed Fish Curry – How Mok	12
Stir Fried Vegetables in Oyster Sauce – Pahd Pak Namman Hoi	11
Sweet & Sour Beef – Priaw Wahn Nuer	15
Sweet & Sour Chicken – Priaw Wahn Gai	12
Sweet & Sour Fish – Priaw Wahn Pla	11
Sweet & Sour Pork – Priaw Wahn Moo	13
Sweet & Sour Prawns – Priaw Wahn Goong	11
Vegetable Green Curry – Gaeng Keo Wan Pak	12

Rice & Noodles

Crispy Fried Egg Noodles with Thai Sauce – Ba-Mee Grob Ranah	24
Egg Fried Rice – Kow Pahd	19
Egg Fried Rice with Cucumber, Coriander & Lemon – Kow Pahd Khai	23
Egg Fried Rice with Pork – Kow Pahd Moo	23
Egg Fried Rice with Prawns – Kow Pahd Goong	23
Fried Egg Noodles – Goi Si Mee	15
Pad Thai with Chicken	24
Pad Thai with Prawns	21
Prawn or Crab Fried Rice – Khao Pad Goong, Pu	21
Steamed Rice – Khao Suay	12
Stir Fried Rice Noodles with Chicken – Phad See Lew Gai	15
Stir Fried Rice Noodles with Pork– Phad See Lew Moo	20
Thai Fried Noodles – Kuaytio Pad Thai	20

Soup

Miso Soup	2

Hot Classics

Chicken Katsu	9
Chicken Katsu Curry	15
Chicken Teriyaki	11
Chicken Yakitori	8
Hairy Prawns	6
Miso Black Cod	7
Prawn Katsu	6
Prawn Yakisoba	8
Pumpkin Korroke	4
Salmon & Aonori Katsu	9
Salmon & Asparagus Yakitori	7
Salmon Teriyaki	9
Seafood Rice	9
Takoyaki	6
Vegetable Firecracker Rice	7
Vegetable Yakisoba	7

Tempura

Assorted	4
Prawn	4
Soft Shell Crab	6
Vegetable	4

ISO

Assorted	6
California Roll	7
Crispy Salmon Skin	6
Crunchy Prawn	7
Eel Dragon Roll	7
Fresh Crab, Cucumber & Tobiko	3
Mini Eel & Cucumber	4
Mini Hamachi & Yuzu Tobiko	3
Poached Salmon & Dill	3
Salmon Dragon Roll	12
Smoked Salmon & Cream Cheese	9
Soft Shell Crab & Rocket	8
Spicy Chicken Katsu	6
Spicy Tuna	2
Vegetable	7
YO! Roll	7

Nigiri

Assorted	2
Eel	5
Hamachi	3

Octopus	2
Prawn	2
Roasted Red Pepper	2
Salmon	1
Seared Beef	8
Tamago	2
Tuna	1

Sashimi

Assorted	3
Coriander Tuna	2
Hamachi	1
Salmon	4
Sesame Salmon	4
Sesame Tuna	2
Shichimi & Dill Salmon	4
Tuna	2

Hand Rolls

California	5
Crispy Duck & Moromi Miso	5
Crispy Salmon Skin	4
Fresh Crab & Avocado	4
Hamachi Ceviche	2
Salmon & Avocado	5
Soft Shell Crab & Rocket	4
Spicy Tuna	2
Vegetable	3

Maki & Futomaki

Asparagus Maki	3
Assorted Fish Maki	8
Avocado Maki	5
Crayfish & Cucumber Futomaki	5
Crispy Duck Futomaki	10
Cucumber Maki	3
Oshinko	3
Red Pepper Maki	2
Salmon Maki	3
Smoked Salmon & Chive Maki	3
Tuna Maki	2
Vegetable Futomaki	5

Gunkan

Ikura	2
Masago	2
Tobiko	2

Coffee Shops

CAUTION: VERY HOT

Decaf

Milk

Shots

Custom

Syrup

Drink

Careful, the beverage you're about to enjoy is extremely hot.

How to order coffee

In the good old days ordering coffee was simple – do you want milk and sugar? These days you need to know how to navigate the menu. Hopefully this will help…

Size Matters: Every coffee shop has its own particular language but asking for small, medium or large usually works. If you're in Starbucks it's tall, grande or venti and in Costa Coffee it's primo, medio and massimo.

Strength: When ordering espresso, it's all about the number of shots – 1 shot (single), 2 shots (doppio), 3 shots (triple), 4 shots (quad). Espresso forms the base of most brewed coffees too – a small cup of brewed coffee usually comes with 1 shot, a medium with 2 and a large with 3 – but you can ask for any number of shots in any size cup.

What kind of milk do you want: Different chains have different names – skinny might mean semi–skimmed or skimmed, it's safest to ask. You could save up to 2 *ProPoints* values just by switching from whole milk to skimmed milk on a regular caffe latte. Whipped cream can add 2 *ProPoints* values to your drink.

Types of brewed coffee…

Espresso – no milk at all

Ristretto – like espresso but stronger (using less water)

Macchiato – just a dab of foamed milk

Cappuccino – one part milk, one part foam (a dry cappuccino is mostly foam)

Latte – lots of milk, a little foam

Mocha – latte with chocolate syrup

Café au lait – brewed coffee with steamed milk

Con panne – espresso with whipped cream

Iced coffee – different chains have different names and options – it's best to ask.

Other things you should know…

Syrups: Chocolate, vanilla, caramel and hazelnut are the most popular and can be added to any drink but watch out – one shot of syrup can add 1 *ProPoints* value. Ask if they have a sugar–free option.

Decaf: Caffeinated coffee is always the default, so if you want decaffeinated, make sure you ask.

Cakes, Biscuits & Desserts

Belgian Chocolate Brownie	9
Biscotti – Almond – Organic	4
Biscotti – Chocolate – Organic	4
Blackcurrant Bio-Yoghurt	6
Blueberry Muffin	12
Brunch Pot – Blueberry (<5% Fat)	4
Brunch Pot – Strawberry	4
Caramel Slice	7
Carrot & Raisin Cake Slice – Organic	7
Chocolate Chip Cookie – Organic	7
Chocolate Coated Coffee Beans	3
Chocolate Coin	3
Chocolate Fudge Cake	17
Cupcake – Banoffee	9
Cupcake – Chocolate	10
Cupcake – Lemon	10
Double Chocolate Brownie, Gluten Free – Organic	9
Granola Bar – Organic	8
Honey Bio-Yoghurt	6
Lemon Drizzle Cake Slice – Organic	7
Lemon Poppy Seed Muffin	12
Luxury Fruit Scone (without butter & jam)	9
Milk Chocolate Bar	6
Milk Chocolate Bar with Hazelnuts	6
Milk Chocolate Chunk Cookie (unwrapped)	9
Mints	1
Oat & Raisin Cookie – Organic	8
Passion Cake	14
Raspberry & White Chocolate Muffin	13
Shortbread – Organic	7
Triple Belgian Chocolate Muffin	14
Triple Chocolate Cookie (unwrapped)	9
White & Dark Chocolate Truffle Cheesecake	15

Coffee & Hot Drinks - Regular

Amaretto Latte (semi-skimmed milk)	5
Cappuccino (semi-skimmed milk)	1
Cappuccino (skimmed milk)	1
Cappuccino (soya milk)	1
Caramelatte (semi-skimmed milk)	13
Chai Latte (semi-skimmed milk)	8
Chai Latte (skimmed milk)	6
Hot Chocolate (semi-skimmed milk)	8
Hot Chocolate (skimmed milk)	7
Hot Chocolate Milano (with whipped cream)	12
Hot Chocolate with Whipped Cream (semi-skimmed milk)	12
Latte (semi-skimmed milk)	2
Latte (skimmed milk)	1

	ProPoints value
Latte (soya milk)	2
Mocha (semi-skimmed milk)	5
Mocha (skimmed milk)	4
Mocha with Whipped Cream (semi-skimmed milk)	9
White Chocolate Mocha (semi-skimmed milk)	10

Cold Drinks

Apple & Mango Juice	3
Apple Juice Carton	3
Banana Frappe Milkshake	12
Double Chocolate Frappe (semi-skimmed milk)	13
Double Chocolate Frappe (skimmed milk)	12
Frappe Latte (semi-skimmed milk)	8
Frappe Latte (skimmed milk)	7
Fresh Orange – 100% Squeezed Juice	3
Iced Chai Latte	13
Iced Latte	3
Mango Fruit Booster	7
Mint Frappe Milkshake	12
Mocha Frappe Latte (semi-skimmed milk)	12
Mocha Frappe Latte (skimmed milk)	12
Orange Juice – Organic	2
Pineapple, Orange & Banana Fruit Booster	6
Pressed Apple – 100% Premium Juice	3
Sicilian Still Lemonade	3
Strawberry & Raspberry Fruit Booster	5
Strawberry Frappe Milkshake	12
Vanilla Frappe Milkshake	12

Crisps & Savouries

Marinated Green Olives	7
Mature Cheddar & Spring Onion Crisps	6
Sea Salt & Balsamic Vinegar Crisps	5
Sea Salt Crisps	5

Panini, Focaccia & Calzone

Bacon Breakfast Panini	8
Chicken & Grilled Vegetable Panini (<5% Fat)	9
Chicken Caesar Panini	14
Ham & Egg Breakfast Panini	10
Ham & Mozzarella Panini	11
Ham, Roasted Mushroom & Mozzarella Focaccia	11
Mozzarella & Meatball Panini	13
Mozzarella & Tomato Calzone	9
Mozzarella, Red Pepper & Roast Tomato Panini	13
Mozzarella, Vine Tomato & Basil Panini	10
Napoli Salami & Mozzarella Panini	10
Pesto Chicken Panini	12
Tuna Melt Panini	11

Pasta & Soup

Carrot & Corriander Soup – Organic	6
Red Pepper Penne (<5% Fat)	7
Sundried Tomato & Basil Soup – Organic	4

Pastries

Almond Pain au Chocolat	9
Cheese Twist	9
Chocolate Twist	9
Croissant – Almond	10
Croissant – Apricot	8
Croissant – Butter	5
Mini Chocolate Panettone	12
Mini Classic Panettone	10
Pain au Chocolat	7
Pain au Raisin	9
Sticky Toffee Muffin	12

Sandwiches & Salads

BLT Bloomer Sandwich	10
Chicken & Orzo Pasta Salad (<5% Fat)	11
Chicken Salad Sandwich	11
Chicken Salsa Wrap (<5% Fat)	9
Falafel Wrap	12
Free Range Egg Mayonnaise Bloomer Sandwich	9
Fruit Salad – Tropical	2
Ham & Cheddar Bloomer Sandwich	12
Mature Cheddar & Pickle Bloomer Sandwich	12
Tuna & Cannelloni Bean Salad with Dressing (<5% Fat)	7
Tuna Salad Bloomer Sandwich	8

Coffee Shops **Costa Coffee**

Coffee

Americano – No Added Milk – All Sizes	0
Babyccino – All Types – Solo	0
Cappuccino – Full Fat Milk – Massimo	3
Cappuccino – Full Fat Milk – Medio	3
Cappuccino – Full Fat Milk – Primo	2
Cappuccino – Skimmed Milk – Massimo	2
Cappuccino – Skimmed Milk – Medio	1
Cappuccino – Skimmed Milk – Primo	1
Cappuccino – Soya Milk – Massimo	2
Cappuccino – Soya Milk – Medio	2
Cappuccino – Soya Milk – Primo	1
Classic Espresso Con Panna – Doppio	3
Classic Espresso Con Panna – Solo	3
Flat White – Full Fat Milk – Primo	5
Flat White – Skimmed or Soya Milk – Primo	3
Latte – Full Fat Milk – Massimo	5
Latte – Full Fat Milk – Primo	3
Latte – Skimmed Milk – Massimo	3
Latte – Skimmed Milk – Primo	1
Latte – Soya Milk – Massimo	5
Latte – Soya Milk – Primo	1
Macchiato – Full Fat Milk – Solo	0
Macchiato – Skimmed Millk – Solo	0
Macchiato – Soya Milk – Solo	0
Mocha – Full Fat Milk – Primo	3
Mocha – Skimmed Milk – Primo	2
Mocha – Soya Milk – Massimo	5
Mocha – Soya Milk – Primo	2
Mocha Flake with Cream – Full Fat Milk – Massimo	10
Mocha Flake with Cream – Full Fat Milk – Medio	8
Mocha Flake with Cream – Full Fat Milk – Primo	7
Mocha Flake with Cream – Skimmed Milk – Massimo	9
Mocha Flake with Cream – Skimmed Milk – Medio	7
Mocha Flake with Cream – Skimmed Milk – Primo	6

Frescatos

Caramel Crunch – Massimo	18
Caramel Crunch – Primo	12
Citrus Fruits – Massimo	10
Citrus Fruits – Primo	6
Coffee – Massimo	9
Coffee – Primo	5
Double Choc Flake – Massimo	19
Double Choc Flake – Medio	15
Double Choc Flake – Primo	12
Mango & Passionfruit – Massimo	7
Mango & Passionfruit – Primo	4
Strawberry Shortcake – Massimo	17

Strawberry Shortcake – Medio	15
Strawberry Shortcake – Primo	12
Summer Berries – Massimo	10
Summer Berries – Medio	8
Summer Berries – Primo	6
Vanilla – Massimo	9
Vanilla – Primo	5

Hot Chocolate

Frothed Milk – Full Fat Milk – Massimo	7
Frothed Milk – Full Fat Milk – Primo	3
Frothed Milk – Skimmed Milk – Massimo	5
Frothed Milk – Skimmed Milk – Primo	3
Frothed Milk – Soya Milk – Massimo	8
Frothed Milk – Soya Milk – Primo	3
Marshmallows & Whipped Cream – Full Fat Milk – Massimo	12
Marshmallows & Whipped Cream – Full Fat Milk – Primo	8
Marshmallows & Whipped Cream – Skimmed Milk – Massimo	9
Marshmallows & Whipped Cream – Skimmed Milk – Primo	7

Iced Coffee

Iced Americano – No Added Milk – All Sizes	0
Iced Cappuccino – Full Fat Milk – Massimo	4
Iced Cappuccino – Full Fat Milk – Primo	2
Iced Cappuccino – Skimmed Milk – Massimo	2
Iced Cappuccino – Skimmed Milk – Primo	1
Iced Cappuccino – Soya Milk – Massimo	3
Iced Cappuccino – Soya Milk – Primo	2
Iced Caramel Latte – Full Fat Milk – Massimo	8
Iced Caramel Latte – Full Fat Milk – Primo	5
Iced Caramel Latte – Skimmed Milk – Massimo	7
Iced Caramel Latte – Skimmed Milk – Primo	4
Iced Caramel Latte – Soya Milk – Massimo	7
Iced Caramel Latte – Soya Milk – Primo	4
Iced Cinnamon Latte – Full Fat Milk – Massimo	8
Iced Cinnamon Latte – Full Fat Milk – Primo	5
Iced Cinnamon Latte – Skimmed Milk – Massimo	7
Iced Cinnamon Latte – Skimmed Milk – Primo	4
Iced Cinnamon Latte – Soya Milk – Massimo	7
Iced Cinnamon Latte – Soya Milk – Primo	4
Iced Gingerbread Latte – Full Fat Milk – Massimo	9
Iced Gingerbread Latte – Full Fat Milk – Primo	5
Iced Gingerbread Latte – Skimmed Milk – Massimo	7
Iced Gingerbread Latte – Skimmed Milk – Primo	4
Iced Gingerbread Latte – Soya Milk – Massimo	7
Iced Gingerbread Latte – Soya Milk – Primo	4
Iced Hazelnut Latte – Full Fat Milk – Massimo	8
Iced Hazelnut Latte – Full Fat Milk – Primo	4
Iced Hazelnut Latte – Skimmed Milk – Massimo	7
Iced Hazelnut Latte – Skimmed Milk – Primo	4

Iced Hazelnut Latte – Soya Milk – Massimo	7
Iced Latte – Full Fat Milk – Massimo	3
Iced Latte – Full Fat Milk – Primo	2
Iced Latte – Skimmed Milk – Massimo	2
Iced Latte – Skimmed Milk – Primo	1
Iced Latte – Soya Milk – Massimo	2
Iced Latte – Soya Milk – Primo	1
Iced Mocha – Full Fat Milk – Massimo	10
Iced Mocha – Full Fat Milk – Primo	4
Iced Mocha – Skimmed Milk – Massimo	8
Iced Mocha – Skimmed Milk – Primo	3
Iced Mocha – Soya Milk – Massimo	9
Iced Mocha – Soya Milk – Primo	3
Iced Vanilla Latte – Full Fat Milk – Massimo	9
Iced Vanilla Latte – Full Fat Milk – Primo	5
Iced Vanilla Latte – Skimmed Milk – Massimo	7
Iced Vanilla Latte – Skimmed Milk – Primo	4
Iced Vanilla Latte – Soya Milk – Massimo	8
Iced Vanilla Latte – Soya Milk – Primo	4

Muffins, Cakes & Traybakes

Blueberry Muffin	13
Breakfast Loaf	12
Carrot Cake	14
Cherry & Almond Muffin	13
Chocolate Cake	19
Chocolate Crunch	11
Chocolate Tiffin Triangle	12
Fruit, Seed, Nut & Honey Bar	9
Lemon & Orange Muffin – Low Fat	9
Linzer Biscuit with Raspberry Jam	9
Mini Muffin Choc	2
Mini Muffin Raspberry & White Choc	2
Panettone al Cioccolato	11
Panettone Tradizionale	9
Raspberry & Almond Bake	12
Triple Chocolate Muffin	15
Winter Fruit Salad	3

Pastries

Almond Croissant	9
Butter Croissant	8
Chocolate Twist	11

Sandwiches

All Day Breakfast Club	16
Arrabiata Chicken Panini	10
Bacon Toastie	9
BLT	12

	ProPoints value
Brie & Tomato Chutney Panini	12
Cheese Ploughman's	12
Chicken & Bacon Club	14
Chicken Caesar Sandwich	8
Emmenthal & Mushroom Flatbread	10
Free Range Egg	9
Green Thai Chicken Flatbread	9
Ham & Cheese Panini	12
Ham & Cheese Toastie	11
Mozzarella, Tomato & Basil Panini	12
New York Deli	11
Ragu Meatball Panini	13
Red Chilli Chicken Panini	9
Spicy Meatball Panini	14
Tuna Melt Panini	12
Tuna Salad	8

Speciality Lattes

Caramel Latte – Full Fat Milk – Massimo	7
Caramel Latte – Full Fat Milk – Primo	4
Caramel Latte – Skimmed Milk – Massimo	4
Caramel Latte – Skimmed Milk – Primo	2
Caramel Latte – Soya Milk – Massimo	7
Caramel Latte – Soya Milk – Primo	3
Cinnamon Latte – Full Fat Milk – Massimo	7
Cinnamon Latte – Full Fat Milk – Primo	4
Cinnamon Latte – Skimmed Milk – Massimo	4
Cinnamon Latte – Skimmed Milk – Primo	2
Cinnamon Latte – Soya Milk – Massimo	7
Cinnamon Latte – Soya Milk – Primo	3
Gingerbread Latte – Full Fat Milk – Massimo	7
Gingerbread Latte – Full Fat Milk – Primo	4
Gingerbread Latte – Skimmed Milk – Massimo	4
Gingerbread Latte – Skimmed Milk – Primo	2
Gingerbread Latte – Soya Milk – Massimo	7
Gingerbread Latte – Soya Milk – Primo	3
Hazelnut Latte – Full Fat Milk – Massimo	7
Hazelnut Latte – Full Fat Milk – Primo	4
Hazelnut Latte – Skimmed Milk – Massimo	4
Hazelnut Latte – Skimmed Milk – Primo	2
Hazelnut Latte – Soya Milk – Massimo	7
Hazelnut Latte – Soya Milk – Primo	3
Vanilla Latte – Full Fat Milk – Massimo	7
Vanilla Latte – Full Fat Milk – Primo	4
Vanilla Latte – Skimmed Milk– Massimo	4
Vanilla Latte – Skimmed Milk – Primo	2
Vanilla Latte – Soya Milk – Massimo	7
Vanilla Latte – Soya Milk – Primo	3

Breakfast

Blueberry Yoghurt with Mixed Seeds	5
Dried Fruit	3
Fruit Salad	0
Granola Topped Greek Yoghurt with Wild Flower Honey	7
Perfect Porridge, Full Fat Milk & Dried Fruit	10
Perfect Porridge, Semi Skimmed Milk & Dried Fruit	9
Perfect Porridge, Skimmed Milk & Dried Fruit	8
Perfect Porridge, Soy Milk & Dried Milk	8
Strawberry Yoghurt with Mixed Seeds	5

Cakes, Pastries & Cheesecakes

All Butter Croissant	8
Almond Croissant	13
Apple & Cinnamon Muffin	12
Banoffee Cake	12
Belgian Chocolate Brownie Gluten Free Fairtrade	9
Blueberry Swirl Cheesecake	13
Chocolate Caramel Shortbread	10
Chocolate Chunk Cookie	11
Chocolate Chunk Shortbread Fairtrade	13
Chocolate Cornflake Square	7
Chocolate Cup Cake	9
Chocolate Muffin with Belgian Choc Sauce Centre	13
Chocolate Velvet Cake	15
Cinnamon Swirl	12
Classic Blueberry Muffin	13
Doughnut Apple Fritter	12
Doughnut Chocolate Cake	11
Doughnut Classic Cake	12
Extremely Fruity Scone	9
Granola Bar	10
Low Fat Apple & Sultana Cake	5
Luxury Fruit Bread	13
Marshmallow Twizzle Chocolate (Dark & White)	4
Marshmallow Twizzle with Coloured Sugar Strands	4
Pain au Chocolat	8
Pain au Raisin	12
Raspberry & Coconut Cake	7
Rise & Shine Muffin	12
Rocky Road	10
Savoury Cheese Pastry	12
Skinny Blueberry Muffin	10
Skinny Lemon & Poppyseed Muffin	11
Skinny Peach & Raspberry Muffin	9
Skinny Stem Ginger Muffin	11
Valencia Orange & Chocolate Cake	5
Victoria Sponge Cupcake	10

Frappuccino Ice Blended

Caramel Cream with Whipped Cream – Tall	9
Caramel Light – Tall	4
Caramel with Whipped Cream – Tall	8
Chocolate Cream Chip with Whipped Cream – Tall	10
Chocolate Cream with Whipped Cream – Tall	9
Coffee – Tall	5
Coffee Light – Tall	3
Espresso – Tall	4
Java Chip with Whipped Cream – Tall	10
Mango Passion Fruit – Tall	4
Mocha Light – Tall	3
Mocha with Whipped Cream – Tall	8
Pomegranate Peach – Tall	6
Raspberry Blackcurrent –Tall	4
Vanilla Coffee with Whipped Cream – Tall	8
Vanilla Cream with Whipped Cream – Tall	8
White Chocolate Mocha with Whipped Cream – Tall	9

Hot Drinks

Caffè Latte – Tall – Semi Skimmed Milk	4
Caffè Latte – Tall – Skimmed Milk	3
Caffè Latte – Tall – Soy	3
Caffè Latte – Tall – Whole Milk	5
Caffè Misto/Café Au Lait – Tall – Semi Skimmed Milk	2
Caffè Misto/Café Au Lait – Tall – Skimmed Milk	1
Caffè Misto/Café Au Lait – Tall – Soy	2
Caffè Misto/Café Au Lait – Tall – Whole Milk	3
Caffè Mocha with Whipped Cream – Tall – Semi Skimmed Milk	8
Caffè Mocha with Whipped Cream – Tall – Skimmed Milk	7
Caffè Mocha with Whipped Cream – Tall – Soy	7
Caffè Mocha with Whipped Cream – Tall – Whole Milk	9
Cappuccino – Tall – Semi Skimmed Milk	2
Cappuccino – Tall – Skimmed Milk	2
Cappuccino – Tall – Soy	2
Cappuccino – Tall – Whole Milk	3
Caramel Macchiato – Tall – Semi Skimmed Milk	5
Caramel Macchiato – Tall – Skimmed Milk	4
Caramel Macchiato – Tall – Soy	4
Caramel Macchiato – Tall – Whole Milk	5
Hazelnut Mocha with Whipped Cream – Tall – Semi Skimmed Milk	9
Hazelnut Mocha with Whipped Cream – Tall – Skimmed Milk	8
Hazelnut Mocha with Whipped Cream – Tall – Soy	8
Hazelnut Mocha with Whipped Cream – Tall – Whole Milk	10
Signature Hot Chocolate with Whipped Cream – Tall – Semi Skimmed Milk	12
Signature Hot Chocolate with Whipped Cream – Tall – Skimmed Milk	12
Signature Hot Chocolate with Whipped Cream – Tall – Soy	12

Signature Hot Chocolate with Whipped Cream – Tall – Whole Milk	**13**
Steamed Milk – Tall – Semi Skimmed Milk	**4**
Steamed Milk – Tall – Skimmed Milk	**3**
Steamed Milk – Tall – Soy	**3**
Steamed Milk – Tall – Whole Milk	**5**
Tazo Chai Tea Latte – Tall – Semi Skimmed Milk	**5**
Tazo Chai Tea Latte – Tall – Skimmed Milk	**4**
Tazo Chai Tea Latte – Tall – Soy	**4**
Tazo Chai Tea Latte – Tall – Whole Milk	**5**
Vanilla Latte – Tall – Semi Skimmed Milk	**5**
Vanilla Latte – Tall – Skimmed Milk	**4**
Vanilla Latte – Tall – Soy	**4**
Vanilla Latte – Tall – Whole Milk	**6**
White Chocolate Mocha with Whipped Cream – Tall – Semi Skimmed Milk	**10**
White Chocolate Mocha with Whipped Cream – Tall – Skimmed Milk	**9**
White Chocolate Mocha with Whipped Cream – Tall – Soy	**9**
White Chocolate Mocha with Whipped Cream – Tall – Whole Milk	**11**

Hot Panini & Savoury Pastries

Cheese & Marmite Panini	**8**
Chicken & Green Pesto Panini	**9**
Croque Monsieur Ham & Cheese Panini	**11**
Dry Cured Ham & Emmental Croissant	**9**
Egg & Bacon & Mushroom Panini	**7**
Falafel Panini	**10**
Italian Mozzarella & Slow Roast Tomato Panini	**11**
Mini Ham & Cheese Toasties	**9**
Roasted Chicken & Tomato Panini	**9**
Steak & Cheese Panini	**11**
Tuna Melt & Mature Cheddar Panini	**12**

Iced Drinks

Iced Caffè Americano – Tall	**0**
Iced Caffè Latte – Tall – Semi Skimmed Milk	**3**
Iced Caffè Latte – Tall – Skimmed Milk	**2**
Iced Caffè Latte – Tall – Soy	**2**
Iced Caffè Latte – Tall – Whole Milk	**3**
Iced Caffè Mocha with Whipped Cream – Tall – Semi Skimmed Milk	**7**
Iced Caffè Mocha with Whipped Cream – Tall – Skimmed Milk	**6**
Iced Caffè Mocha with Whipped Cream – Tall – Soy	**7**
Iced Caffè Mocha with Whipped Cream – Tall – Whole Milk	**7**
Iced Caramel Macchiato – Tall – Semi Skimmed Milk	**5**
Iced Caramel Macchiato – Tall – Skimmed Milk	**4**
Iced Caramel Macchiato – Tall – Soy	**4**
Iced Caramel Macchiato – Tall – Whole Milk	**5**
Iced Coffee – Tall	**0**
Iced Hazelnut Mocha with Whipped Cream – Tall – Semi Skimmed Milk	**9**
Iced Hazelnut Mocha with Whipped Cream – Tall – Skimmed Milk	**9**

Iced Hazelnut Mocha with Whipped Cream – Tall – Soy	9
Iced Hazelnut Mocha with Whipped Cream – Tall – Whole Milk	10
Iced Tazo Chai Tea Latte – Tall – Semi Skimmed Milk	5
Iced Tazo Chai Tea Latte – Tall – Skimmed Milk	4
Iced Tazo Chai Tea Latte – Tall – Soy	4
Iced Tazo Chai Tea Latte – Tall – Whole Milk	5
Iced Vanilla Latte – Tall – Semi Skimmed Milk	4
Iced Vanilla Latte – Tall – Skimmed Milk	3
Iced Vanilla Latte – Tall – Soy	3
Iced Vanilla Latte – Tall – Whole Milk	4

Nibbles

After Coffee Mints (Tin of 50)	11
Dolcetto al Cacao	4
Fairtrade Chocolate Bar – Milk	7
Fairtrade Chocolate Bar – Dark	7
Fruit & Nut Bar – Cranberry, Pumpkin Seed & Blueberry	6
Fruit & Nut Bar – Mango, Pistachio & Cashew	6
Fruit & Nut Bar – Peanut Pecan, Cherry & Maple Syrup	7
Fruit & Oat Cookie	6
Gold Coins	3
Lollipops	1
Mature Cheddar & Spring Onion Crisps	7
Nut Mix	11
Oriental Spice	7
Roasted Almonds	27
Sea Salt Crisps	7
Sea Salt & Cider Vinegar Crisps	7

Sandwiches, Salads & Wraps

BLT	13
Chicken with Red Pesto Pasta Salad	10
Free Range Egg Mayo	10
Ham, Mushroom & Tomato Crêpe	4
Houmous with Vegetable Sticks	3
Moroccan Couscous & Roasted Vegetable	8
Oak Smoked Salmon & Soft Cheese	10
Roasted Chicken & Beechwood Smoked Bacon	13
Roasted Chicken Salsa Wrap	10
Roasted Chicken with Herb Mayonnaise	9
Three Bean & Cheese Wrap	12
Toasted Club Sandwich	14
Tomato Mozzarella Pasta Salad	5
Tuna & Three Bean Salad	9
Tuna Mayonnaise Gluten Free	12

Syrups & Toppings

Bar Mocha Syrup – per Pump	1
Flavoured Syrup – per 2 Pumps	1
Whipped Cream Topping – Cold or Hot Tall Beverage	2

Fish, Fish & Chip Shops

Starters

Caviar (2 tablespoons)	1
Calamari	15
Dressed Crab	12
Fishcakes (2)	11
Fish Soup (without Cream)	7
Garlic Prawns	12
Garlic Sardines	11
Lobster Bisque (without Cream)	6
Mussels in White Wine & Cream	14
Prawn Cocktail	12
Salmon Mousse/Pâté	9
Spicy King Prawns	6
Whitebait	15

Grilled/Baked/Steamed

Fillet of Salmon	9
Lobster (half)	3
Whole Dover Sole	5
Whole Lemon Sole	4
Whole Plaice	4
Whole Skate Wing	5
Whole Trout	8

Deep Fried

Cod in Batter	16
Haddock in Batter	16
Hake in Batter	16
Plaice in Breadcrumbs	16
Scampi in Breadcrumbs	13
Skate in Batter	15

Sauces

Bonne Femme	9
Hollandaise	11
Parsley	6
Peppercorn	7

Main Courses

Bouillabaisse with Rouille	15
Cod in Parsley Sauce	13
Fish Pie	17
Grilled Swordfish with Prawn Sauce	11
Grilled Tuna Steak in Lemon Butter	14
King Prawns with Garlic Butter	12
Lobster Thermidor	16
Poached Halibut Bonne Femme	15
Poached Salmon with Prawn Sauce	12
Seafood Platter	12

Harry's Starters

Battered Chicken Dippers	7
Cajun Prawns	9
Crispy Coated Mushrooms	14
Harry's Full House Combo Platter (Half)	15
Prawn Cocktail	9

Harry's Famous Fish & Chips (one serving of chips)

Cajun Prawns	21
Cod Fillet, Regular	23
Fillet of Plaice	27
Fish Bites	21
Haddock Fillet, Regular	22
Wholetail Scampi	22

More Tasty Mains

Battered Chicken & Chips	19
Battered Chicken & Wholetail Scampi with Chips	26
Battered Chicken in a Bun with Chips	23
Harry's Famous Fish in a Bun with Chips	21
Harry's Fresh Salad	16
Sausage & Mash	18

Sauces, Dips & Sides

Baked Beans	3
BBQ Dip	2
Chips	12
Creamy Mash Potato	7
Garden Peas	2
Garlic Mayonnaise Dip	4
Mushy Peas	2
Onion Rings	6
Potato Wedges	5
Salad, No Dressing	0
Sweet Chilli Dip	2

Delicious Desserts

Chocolate Puddle Pudding	20
Deluxe Dairy Ice Cream, per Scoop	6
Homemade Bread & Butter Pudding	18
Lemon Meringue Pie	11
Strawberry Shortcake Split Cheesecake	14
Sticky Toffee Pudding	15
Swiss Mountain Chocolate Chunk Cheesecake	20

Food on the Go

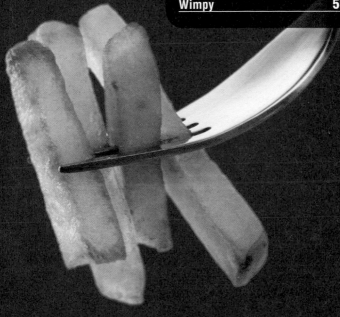

Bagels

Bran	7
Cheese	8
Cinnamon & Raisin	7
Granary	8
Health Seed	8
Honey Sunflower	8
Onion Multiseed	8
Plain	8
Poppy	8
Pretzel	8
Rye	7
Sesame	8
Wholemeal	7

Fish & Meat

Crispy Bacon	4
Cumberland Sausage	4
Grilled Chicken	1
Ham	1
Salt Beef	2
Smoked Salmon	2
Tuna Flakes	1
Turkey	1

Salads

All Vegetable Salad Ingredients	0
Sun Sweet Tomato, Sweet Pepper	1

Spreads & Cheeses

Banana	1
Butter	1
Cheddar Cheese	4
Cream Cheese, Full Fat	8
Cream Cheese, Low Fat	3
Emmental/Swiss Cheese	4
Guacamole	2
Houmous	6
Marmalade	3
Marmite	1
Mozzarella	3
Nutella	4
Peanut Butter	5
Shaved Parmesan	2
Strawberry Jam	2

Delicious

Sandwiches & Salads

Bacon, Lettuce & Tomato	11
Brie, Tomato & Rocket	12
Cheese & Onion	12
Cheese Ploughman's	11
Cheese Salad Baguette	14
Chicken & Bacon	10
Chicken Caesar Wrap	10
Chicken Triple: Chicken Salad, Chicken & Bacon, Chicken & Sweetcorn	13
Egg & Bacon Sub	11
Egg Mayonnaise & Cress	9
Falafel Wrap	13
Ham & Emmental Cheese	13
Ham & Mustard	9
Ham Hock & Tomato Sub Roll	9
Mexican Style Bean Wrap	12
Pesto Pasta Salad	12
Prawn Mayonnaise	9
Salmon & Cucumber Sub Roll	8
Salmon & Dill	10
Sandwich Triple: Ham & Cheese, Tuna & Sweetcorn, Egg Mayonnaise	13
Southern Fried Chicken Wrap	11
Tomato & Basil Chicken Pasta Salad	12
Three of the Best Sandwich Triple: Chicken Salad, Prawn Mayo & BLT	12
Tuscan Style Vegetables	9
Vintage Cheddar Cheese Plait	8

Sweet & Savoury Treats

Belgian Dark Chocolate	11
Belgian Milk Chocolate with Blueberries	10
Belgian Milk Chocolate	11
Caramel & Mixed Nut Cereal Bar	6
Handmade Bakewell Slice	7
Hand Finished Caramel Shortbread	8
Hand Finished Lemon Drizzle Cake	7
Hazelnut Belgian Chocolate	7
Lightly Salted Handcooked Vegetable Crisps	4
Raspberry & Vanilla Oatie Smoothie	6
Refreshingly Still Pink Lemonade	4
Roast Chicken with Lemon & Herbs Handcooked Crisps	5
Sour Cream & Black Pepper Handcooked Crisps	5
Spanish Chorizo Handcooked Crisps	5
Strawberry & Blackcurrant Fruit Crush	4
Strawberry & Raspberry Smoothie	4

Tropical Fruit & Mixed Nut Cereal Bar	6
Vanilla Bean & Honey Smoothie	8
White Chocolate with Apricots & Raisins	8

Shapers

Sandwiches, Salads & Sushi

Barbecue Chicken Wrap	8
Cheese & Bean Wrap	8
Chicken & Pesto Sandwich	9
Chicken & Stuffing Sandwich	8
Chicken Fajita Wrap	8
Chicken, No Mayo Sandwich	8
Crayfish & Rocket	8
Egg Mayonnaise & Cress Sandwich	8
Falafel Flatbread	7
Honey & Mustard Chicken Pasta Salad	9
Houmous & Mixed Vegetables Wrap	7
Mature Cheddar & Fruit Chutney Sandwich	9
Prawn Mayonnaise Sandwich	8
Red Thai Chicken Wrap	6
Roast Chicken Salad Sandwich	7
Salmon & Cucumber Sandwich	8
Soft Cheese, Roasted Vegetables & Sunblush Tomato Sandwich	7
Spicy Mexican Flatbread	7
Sushi Rolls	6
Sushi Rolls – Veggie	6
Sushi Selection – Mini	4
Sweet Chilli Chicken Wrap	7
Tex Mex Chicken & Salsa Flatbread	7
Three Bean Salad	4
Tuna & Cucumber Sandwich	7
Tuna & Sweetcorn	8
Tzatziki Chicken Sandwich	8
Vegetable Pakora Sandwich	8

Sweet & Savoury Treats

Apple, Strawberry & Kiwi Fruit Probiotic Yogurt Snack	2
Black Cherry Yogurt	2
Blackcurrant Granola	5
Blueberry & Yogurt Nougat Bar	2
Blueberry Yogurt	3
Chargrilled Chicken Crinkles	3
Chocolate Caramel Bar	3
Chocolate Coffee Nougat Bar	3
Chocolate Mint Nougat Bar	3
Crispy Bacon Bites	3
Crispy Caramel Bar	3
Crunchy Onion Rings	2

	ProPoints value
Double Chocolate Bar	3
Greek Style Yogurt & Forest Fruits	2
Jumbo Raisins & Sultanas	4
Lightly Salted Potato Tubes	3
Manhattan Mini Pretzels	3
Mini Chocolate Chip Cookies	4
Mini Raspberry & White Chocolate Cookies	4
Orange, Mango & Lime Fruit Crush	4
Raspberry Granola	5
Raspberry Yogurt	3
Rhubarb Yogurt	2
Salt & Vinegar Chipsticks	3
Salt & Vinegar Crispy Discs	3
Salt & Vinegar Crunchy Sticks	3
Sour Cream & Chive Crispy Discs	3
Strawberry Nougat Bar	3
Strawberry Yogurt	3
Strawberry, Cornflake & Yogurt Bar	2
Thai Chilli Crunchies	3
Zingy Rhubarb Yogurt	2

Breakfast

Big Beefy with Heinz Ketchup	19
Big Beefy with HP Sauce	19
BK Bacon & Egg Butty/Bap with Heinz Ketchup	10
BK Bacon & Egg Butty/Bap with HP Sauce	10
BK Bacon Butty/Bap with Heinz Ketchup	6
BK Bacon Butty/Bap with HP Sauce	6
Breakfast in Bread with Heinz Ketchup	16
Breakfast in Bread with HP Sauce	16
Egg & Cheese Butty/Bap with Heinz Ketchup	8
Egg & Cheese Butty/Bap with HP Sauce	8
Hash Browns, Regular	9
Hash Browns, Large	11
Mini Pancakes with Maple Syrup, Regular	7
Mini Pancakes with Maple Syrup, Large	10
Sausage & Egg Butty/Bap with Heinz Ketchup	12
Sausage & Egg Butty/Bap with HP Sauce	12
Sausage Butty/Bap with Heinz Ketchup	8
Sausage Butty/Bap with HP Sauce	8

Chicken, Fish & Veggie

BK Veggie Bean Burger	16
Chicken Bites	8
Chicken Royale	16
Chicken Royale with Cheese	19
Ocean Catch	13
Piri Piri Chicken Sandwich	5
Sweet Chilli Chicken Royale	14

Flame-Grilled Burgers

Angus Burger	15
Bacon Double Cheeseburger	13
Cheeseburger	8
Double Angus Burger	21
Double Cheeseburger	12
Double Whopper	24
Double Whopper with Cheese	26
Hamburger	7
Smoked Bacon & Cheddar Angus Burger	18
Smoked Bacon & Cheddar Double Angus Burger	24
Whopper	17
Whopper Junior	9
Whopper Junior with Cheese	10
Whopper with Cheese	19
XL Bacon Double Cheeseburger	25

Salads

| Flame-Grilled Chicken Salad | 3 |
| Garden Salad | 1 |

Sides & Sauces

BBQ Sauce Dip Pot	1
French Dressing Sachet	0
Fries, Small	6
Fries, Regular	10
Fries, Large	16
Fries, Super	24
Hash Browns, Regular	9
Honey & Mustard Dressing Sachet	1
Ketchup Sachet	0
Mayonnaise Sachet	2
Onion Rings, Regular	13
Onion Rings, Large	19
Onion Rings, Super	26
Sweet Chilli Sauce Dip Pot	3

Desserts & Shakes

BK Fusions Strawberry Cheesecake	10
BK Shake Chocolate, Regular	13
BK Shake Chocolate, Large	17
BK Shake Strawberry, Regular	12
BK Shake Strawberry, Large	17
BK Shake Vanilla, Regular	11
BK Shake Vanilla, Large	15

Beverages

Cappuccino – Regular	2
Coca Cola – Small	4
Coca Cola – Regular	5
Coca Cola – Large	7
Coca Cola – Super	11
Fanta Orange – Small	3
Fanta Orange – Regular	4
Fanta Orange – Large	7
Fanta Orange – Super	10
Latte – Regular	2
Sprite – Small	3
Sprite – Regular	4
Sprite – Large	6
Sprite – Super	9
Tea, with Milk, No Sugar, Regular	1

Breakfast

Bacon Butty (Hot Toasted English Muffin) Regular	7
Bacon Butty (Hot Toasted English Muffin) Large	15
Banana, Honey & Grapenuts	10
Belgian Chocolate Muffin	15
Blueberry Muffin, Low Fat	8
Carrot, Bran & Nut Muffin	14
Cheese Twist	9
Cinnamon Whirl	11
Croissant	8
Croissant – Almond	13
Croissant – Chocolate	12
Cumberland Sausage (Hot Toasted English Muffin)	8
Egg, Mushroom & Cheddar (Hot Toasted English Muffin)	8
Eggs Benedict (Hot Toasted English Muffin)	8
Full English Breakfast (Hot Toasted English Muffin)	19
Full Scottish Breakfast (Hot Toasted English Muffin)	19
Ham & Jarlsberg Croissant	9
Iced Ginger & Cinnamon Muffin	13
Maple Pecan Plait	12
Pain au Chocolate	9
Plain Porridge, 8oz	4
Plain Porridge, 12oz	6
Porridge with Apple & Blackberry Compote, 8oz	6
Porridge with Apple & Blackberry Compote, 12oz	8
Porridge with Banana, 8oz	5
Porridge with Banana, 12oz	7
Porridge with Banana & Maple Syrup, 8oz	6
Porridge with Banana & Maple Syrup, 12oz	8
Porridge with Maple Syrup, 8oz	5
Porridge with Maple Syrup, 12oz	7
Swiss Bircher Muesli	9
Yogurt & Granola	10
Yogurt with Apple & Blackberry Compote	10
Yogurt with Blueberry & Pomegranate	4
Yogurt with Muesli & Mixed Berries	8
Yogurt, Apple & Blackberry (Small)	4

Cakes, Cookies & Slices

Banana & Walnut Cake	8
Caramel, Fruit & Oat Cookie	8
Carrot Cake	9
Chocolate Brownie	9
Chocolate Cake	9
Chocolate Cookie	13
Chocolate Cupcake	8
Coconut Slice	10
Cranberry & Orange Cake	9
Honey & Chilli Nuts	12
Honey Toasted Nut & Fruit	6

	ProPoints value
Lemon Cake	9
Milk Chocolate Tiffin	9
Muesli Cookie	10
Nougat	4
Strawberry Cupcake	8
Toffee Bar	8
Toffee Waffles	9
Vanilla Cupcake (Pink/Green)	8
Vanilla Fudge	11

Dessert Pots & Fruit Salads

Banoffee Pie	11
Big Fruit Salad	4
Blueberry & Raspberry Cheesecake	10
Chunky Chocolate Fudge	12
Lemon Cheesecake	13
Mango, Pineapple & Lime Fruit Salad	2

Soups

Cauliflower & Cheese (Small)	9
Cauliflower & Cheese (Big)	12
Chicken & Garden Vegetable Broth (Small)	4
Chicken & Garden Vegetable Broth (Big)	5
Chicken Laksa (Small)	7
Chicken Laksa (Big)	10
Chicken Pot Pie (Small)	8
Chicken Pot Pie (Big)	10
Chicken, Leek & Bacon Risotto (Small)	9
Chicken, Leek & Bacon Risotto (Big)	11
Chorizo & Chickpea (Small)	8
Chorizo & Chickpea (Big)	10
Chunky Minestrone with Pesto (Small)	5
Chunky Minestrone with Pesto (Big)	7
Cream of Corn (Small)	8
Cream of Corn (Big)	11
Creamy Chicken (Small)	7
Creamy Chicken (Big)	9
French Onion (Small)	5
French Onion (Big)	6
Garden Vegetable (Small)	4
Garden Vegetable (Big)	6
Goan Potato (Small)	6
Goan Potato (Big)	8
Gujarati Red Dal with Riata (Small)	3
Gujarati Red Dal with Riata (Big)	4
Hungarian Goulash (Small)	6
Hungarian Goulash (Big)	7
Italian Ragu & Pasta (Small)	5
Italian Ragu & Pasta (Big)	6
Leek, Potato & Chive (Small)	4
Leek, Potato & Chive (Big)	6

Mexican Bean (Small)	5
Mexican Bean (Big)	6
Old Fashioned Chicken & Egg Noodles (Small)	2
Old Fashioned Chicken & Egg Noodles (Big)	3
Roasted Red Pepper & Tomato (Small)	2
Roasted Red Pepper & Tomato (Big)	3
Roast Pumpkin (Small)	4
Roast Pumpkin (Big)	6
Slow Roasted Tomato (Small)	7
Slow Roasted Tomato (Big)	9
Smokey Bacon & Lentil (Small)	3
Smokey Bacon & Lentil(Big)	4
Spicy Tomato & Basil (Small)	2
Spicy Tomato & Basil (Big)	3
Sweet Potato & Chilli (Small)	7
Sweet Potato & Chilli (Big)	10
Texan Chilli con Carne (Small)	8
Texan Chilli con Carne (Big)	10
Thai Butternut Squash (Small)	4
Thai Butternut Squash (Big)	5
Thai Green Chicken Curry (Small)	7
Thai Green Chicken Curry (Big)	9
Tomato, Pancetta & Mascarpone (Small)	4
Tomato, Pancetta & Mascarpone (Big)	6
Toulouse Sausage, Butter Bean & Lentil (Small)	5
Toulouse Sausage, Butter Bean & Lentil (Big)	7
Wild Forest Mushroom (Small)	4
Wild Forest Mushroom (Big)	5

Pies

Beef & Stilton	18
Cheddar Cheese, Potato & Onion	18
Chicken & Mushroom	18
Chicken, Ham & Leek	20
Goat's Cheese & Sweet Potato	18
Steak & Ale	18

Salads, Sandwiches, Baguettes & Wraps

Bacon, Lettuce & Tomato Sandwich	14
Bombay Bhaji Sandwich	10
Brie, Tomato & Basil Baguette	15
Chargrilled Vegetable & Mozzarella Toastie	15
Cheese, Spring Onion & Salad Cream Sandwich	14
Chicken & Bacon Sandwich	14
Chicken Salad Sandwich	9
Chicken, Avocado & Basil Sandwich	16
Chicken, Basil Pesto & Pine Nuts Sandwich (Wheat Free)	16
Chorizo & Peppers Baguette	17
Chunky Free Range Egg Mayonnaise & Cress	13

Club Sandwich	21
Coriander & Lemon Houmous Sandwich	11
Coriander & Lemon Houmous Sandwich (Wheat Free)	15
Coronation Chicken Sandwich	16
Crayfish, Lemon & Rocket Sandwich	9
Egg, Spinach & Chargrilled Peppers Sandwich	15
Fish Salad	9
Free Range Egg Mayo & Bacon Sandwich	16
Free Range Egg Mayo & Cress Sandwich	11
Free Range Egg Mayo & Cress Sandwich (Wheat Free)	15
Ham & Jarlsberg Baguette	17
Ham, Brie & Cranberry Baguette	22
Ham, Cheddar & Real Ale Pickle Sandwich	15
Lemon Chicken & Black Pepper Sandwich (Wheat Free)	14
Mature Farmhouse Cheddar & Branston Baguette	19
Mediterranean Tuna Sandwich (Wheat Free)	13
Mexican Chicken Wrap	11
Moroccan Falafel Wrap	10
Mozzarella & Slow Roast Tomato Sandwich	13
New York Club Sandwich	13
New York Sandwich (Wheat Free)	16
Peking Duck Wrap	12
Prawn Cocktail (Side Salad)	9
Prawn Cocktail Sandwich	12
Prawn Cocktail Sandwich (Wheat Free)	15
Rainbow Sprouted (Side Salad)	9
Roast Beef & Rocket Baguette	18
Simply Ham & Cheese Toastie	21
Smoked Chicken & Basil Toastie	21
Smoked Chicken, Tomato & Pesto Sandwich	13
Smoked Ham & Mature Cheddar Sandwich (Wheat Free)	17
Spicy Chicken Noodles Salad	10
Spicy Crayfish Noodles Salad	10
Steak & Cheese Melt Toastie	23
Superfood Salad	14
Superfood Sandwich	14
Thai Chicken Baguette	17
Thai Citrus Chicken Sandwich	11
Thai Noodle Salad	15
Tuna & Cheddar Melt Toastie	21
Tuna & Cucumber Baguette	17
Tuna & Red Onion Sandwich	8
Tuna, Ginger & Wasabi Sandwich	14
Turkey & Cranberry Sandwich	10
Vegetarian Salad	6
Very Small New York Club Sandwich	7
Very Small Tuna & Red Onion Sandwich	4
Very Small Turkey & Cranberry Sandwich	5

Baguettes

Cheese & Ham	16
Chicken Club	18
Chicken Pesto	14
Chicken Tikka	13
Egg Mayonnaise & Tomato	14
Tuna Crunch	15

Bread Packs

Cheese Savoury	12
Chicken & Stuffing	13
Chicken Salad	13
Chicken Salad with Reduced Fat Mayonnaise	10
Egg Mayonnaise	11
Tuna Mayonnaise	12
Tuna with Reduced Fat Mayonnaise & Cucumber	9

Bloomers

Chicken, Bacon & Sweetcorn on Brown	18
Chicken, Bacon & Sweetcorn on White	16
Chicken & Mango on Brown	15
Chicken & Mango on White	14
Egg & Bacon on Brown	17
Egg & Bacon on White	18
Ham, Cheese & Pickle on Brown	17
Ham, Cheese & Pickle on White	16
Tuna Crunch on Brown	14
Tuna Crunch on White	13

Freshly Baked Savouries

Cheese & Onion Pasty	10
Cheese & Tomato Pizza	9
Chicken Bake	12
Cornish Pasty	13
Sausage, Bean & Cheese Melt	13
Sausage Roll	9
Steak Bake	11

Oval Bites

Chargrill Chicken	11
Cheese Ploughman's	12
Ham Salad	8
Mexican Chicken	10

Original Recipe Chicken

Breast	7
Drumstick	4
Rib	6
Thigh	6
Wing	4

Sandwiches

Fillet Burger	12
Fillet Tower Burger	17
Mini Fillet Burger	7
Toasted Salsa Twister	14
Toasted Twister	14
Zinger Burger	13
Zinger Tower Burger	18

Salads & Snacks

Caesar Dressing	3
Low Fat Vinaigrette Dressing	1
Mini Fillet (Not in a Bun)	3
Original Recipe Chicken Salad (No Dressing)	7
Popcorn Chicken – Large	13
Popcorn Chicken – Regular	8
Zinger Salad (No Dressing)	8

Extras, Sauces & Sides

BBQ Beans – Regular	3
BBQ Beans – Large	5
Coleslaw – Regular	4
Coleslaw – Large	8
Corn-Cobette	4
Crispy Strip	3
Fries – Regular	7
Fries – Large	10
Gravy – Regular	2
Gravy – Large	4
Hot Wings (Per Wing)	3

Drinks

7up – Regular	3
7up – Large	5
Apple Tango – Regular	3
Apple Tango – Large	4
Orange Tango – Regular	2
Orange Tango – Large	1
Pepsi – Regular	4
Pepsi – Large	5

Doughnuts

Chocolate Iced Custard Filled	8
Chocolate Iced Glazed	7
Chocolate Iced with Crème Flavour Filling	9
Chocolate Iced with Sprinkles	8
Cinnamon Apple Filled	8
Glazed Chocolate Cake	9
Glazed Cruller	7
Glazed Lemon Filled	8
Glazed Raspberry Flavour	8
Glazed with Crème Flavour Filling	9
Maple Flavour Iced	8
Original Glazed	6
Powdered Blueberry Filled	8
Powdered Strawberry Filled	7
Vanilla Cake	9

Drinks

Cappuccino – Small	1
Latte – Small	1

Breakfast

Bacon & Egg McMuffin	9
Bacon, Egg & Cheese Bagel	12
Bacon Roll with Brown Sauce or Tomato Ketchup	9
Bagel with Strawberry Jam	7
Big Breakfast	16
Butter Portion	2
Double Bacon & Egg McMuffin	11
Double Sausage & Egg McMuffin	15
Flora Portion	2
Hash Brown	3
Oatso Simple, Plain	5
Pancakes & Sausage	12
Pancakes & Syrup	14
Pancake Syrup	5
Philadelphia Light	1
Sausage & Egg McMuffin	11
Sausage, Egg & Cheese Bagel	15
Strawberry Jam	1
Toasted Bagel	6

Beef

Big Mac	13
Big Tasty	23
Big Tasty with Bacon	24
Cheeseburger	8
Double Cheeseburger	12
Hamburger	7
Quarter Pounder with Cheese	13

Chicken

CBO: Chicken, Bacon & Onion	16
Chicken Legend with Bacon – Spicy Tomato Salsa	15
Chicken Legend with Cool Mayo	15
Chicken Legend with Spicy Tomato Salsa	14
Chicken McNuggets (6 pieces)	7
Chicken McNuggets (9 pieces)	11
Chicken Selects (3 pieces)	10
Chicken Selects (5 pieces)	16
Chicken Tikka Snack Wrap	7
Mayo Chicken	9
McChicken Sandwich	10
Ranch Snack Wrap	9

Fish & Vegetarian

Filet-O-Fish	9
Fish Fingers	5
Vegetable Deluxe	11

Salads Plus

Crispy Chicken & Bacon Salad (No Dressing/No Crackers)	9
Crispy Chicken Salad (No Bacon)	7
Garden Side Salad	0
Grilled Chicken & Bacon Salad	4
Grilled Chicken Salad (No Bacon)	3

Fries & Dips

BBQ or Tomato Ketchup Dip Pot	1
French Fries, Small	6
French Fries, Medium	9
French Fries, Large	13
Low Fat Balsamic Dressing	1
Low Fat Caesar Salad Dressing	2
Smokey BBQ Dip	2
Sour Cream & Chive Dip	5
Sweet & Sour Dip or Sweet Curry Dip	1

Desserts & Treats

Apple Pie	7
Belgian Bliss Brownie	11
Double Chocolate Muffin	12
Fruit Bag	0
Ice Cream Cone with Cadbury Flake	6
Low Fat Blueberry Muffin	8
McFlurry, Cadbury Creme Egg	11
McFlurry, Crunchie, Dairy Milk or Smarties	9
McFlurry, Wispa	11
Strawberry Sundae	10
Sugar Donut	6
Toffee Sundae	10

Drinks & Shakes

Cappuccino, Regular	2
Cappuccino, Large	3
Coca-Cola, Small	3
Coca-Cola, Large	6
Coffee White, Regular	1
Coffee White, Large	1
Fanta Orange, Small	3
Fanta Orange, Large	6
Hot Chocolate, Regular	4
Hot Chocolate, Large	5
Latte, Regular	4
Latte, Large	5
Milkshake, Banana or Strawberry, Large	15
Milkshake, Chocolate or Vanilla, Large	14

Bitesize Cookies

Double Chocolate	3
M&M	3
Milk Chocolate	3
White Chocolate	3

Classic Cookies

Apple & White Chocolate	5
Apricot & Almond	5
Cherry	5
Chocolate & Orange	5
Cranberry & White Chocolate	5
Double Chocolate	5
Fruit 'n' Nut	5
Ginger	5
Milk Chocolate	5
Oatmeal & Raisin	5
Peanut & Milk Chocolate	5
Plain Chocolate	5
Raspberry & White Chocolate	5
Strawberries 'n' Cream	5
Toffee & Milk Chocolate	5
Toffee Popcorn	5
White Chocolate	5

Super Gourmet Cookies

Milk Chocolate	13
Plain Chocolate	13
Raspberry & White Chocolate	11
Triple Chocolate	12
White Chocolate	13

Muffins & Cakes

Banana & Toffee Muffin	18
Blueberry Muffin	17
Cappuccino Muffin	21
Cherry & Almond Muffin	17
Chocolate Fudge Brownie Cake	11
Double Chocolate Muffin	22
Lemon Meringue Muffin	19
Milk Chocolate Chunk Muffin	21
Muesli Muffin	19
Raspberry & White Chocolate Muffin	19
Reduced Fat Mixed Berry Muffin	13

Sandwiches

All Day Breakfast	15
Beech-Smoked BLT	14
Chicken Avocado	13
Chicken Pistachio	12
Classic Ham & Eggs Bloomer	15
Classic Super Club	15
Club Mezze	10
Coronation Chicken	14
Egg & Bacon Croissant	11
Egg Florentine	14
Falafel & Chunky Humous	13
Free Range Egg Mayo	12
Ham & Italian Cheese	13
Ham, Bacon & Cheese Croissant	10
Herb Chicken & Rocket	12
Humous & Roasted Pepper	13
Mature Cheddar & Pickle	16
Mozzarella Pesto Bloomer	15
Mozzarella & Pistachio	15
Mozzarella & Tomato Croissant	10
New York Cheddar Club	17
Pole & Line Caught Tuna	12
Pret Ploughman's	16
Pret Sausage Roll	13
Pret's Famous All Day Breakfast	18
Sausage & Bacon Bloomer	17
Scottish Smoked Salmon	9
Simple Chicken Caesar	14
Simply Ham & Mustard	11
Slim Pret – All Day Breakfast	8
Slim Pret – Beech–Smoked BLT	7
Slim Pret – Chicken Avocado	6
Slim Pret – Classic Super Club	7
Slim Pret – Crayfish & Rocket	5
Slim Pret – Mature Cheddar & Pickle	8
Slim Pret – Pole & Line Caught Tuna	6
Smoked Salmon & Free Range Egg	12
Sustainable Salmon Niçoise	13
The New York Bloomer	14
Wild Crayfish & Rocket	10

Baguettes & Salad Wraps

Avocado & Herb Salad Wrap	13
Brie, Tomato & Whole Leaf Basil Baguette	12
Chicken Tikka Masala Hot Wrap	11
Chilli Beef Hot Wrap	11
Egg Mayo & Bacon Breakfast Baguette	9
Free Range Egg Mayo & Bacon Breakfast Baguette	10
Free Range Egg Mayo & Roasted Tomato Breakfast Baguette	9

Full Size Egg & Bacon Breakfast Baguette	15
Full Size Egg & Smoked Salmon Breakfast Baguette	13
Hoisin Duck Wrap	12
Italian Meatballs	7
Italian Pizza Hot Wrap	10
Italian Prosciutto Artisan Baguette	17
Jalapeño Chicken Hot Wrap	12
Mozzarella & Pesto Hot Artisan Baguette	16
Pole & Line Caught Tuna Baguette	13
Posh Cheddar & Pickle Baguette	21
Pret's Chicken Caesar Baguette	14
Pret's Posh Bacon Baguette	16
Slim Pret – Brie, Tomato & Whole Leaf Basil Baguette	6
Slim Pret – Italian Proscuitto Artisan Baguette	9
Slim Pret – Pole & Line Caught Tuna Baguette	7
Slim Pret – Posh Cheddar & Pickle Artisan Baguette	11
Slim Pret – Pret's Chicken Caesar Baguette	7
Slim Pret – Topside of Beef & Mustard Artisan Baguette	7
Slim Pret – Wiltshire Cured Ham & Greve Baguette	7
Smoked Salmon & Free-Range Egg Breakfast Baguette	10
Spicy Falafel Melt Hot Wrap	13
Topside of Beef & Mustard on Artisan	14
Wiltshire Cured Ham & Greve Baguette	15

Sushi, Salads & Soups

Artisan Soup Bread	5
Chicken & Mushroom Soup	7
Chicken Caesar Salad	8
Chorizo & Butterbean Soup	5
Deluxe Sushi	10
Edamame Bowl	2
Grilled Pepper Salad	11
Lentil & Bacon Soup	8
Maki & Nigiri	8
Malaysian Chicken Soup	5
Mezze Salad	7
Moroccan Chicken Soup	6
Mushroom Risotto Soup	6
No Bread Crayfish & Avocado	5
No Bread Falafel	4
Pole & Line Caught Tuna Niçoise Salad	5
Pret Classic Tomato Soup	4
Pret Tapas Salad	9
Sag-Aloo Soup	7
Spinach & Nutmeg Soup	8
Super (Duper) Health & Humous Salad	10
Thai Corn (on the Cob) Soup	6
Vegetable Sushi	8
Veggie Bento Box	11
Wild Crayfish & Smoked Salmon Salad	4
Winter Vegetable Soup	7

Bakery, Cakes & Slices

Apple & Sultana Muffin	14
Apple Card Box Cake	8
Banana Card Box Cake	10
Carrot Card Box Cake	11
Chocolate & Oat Cookie	9
Chocolate Brownie	7
Chocolate Card Box Cake	10
Croissant – Almond	10
Croissant – Chocolate	12
Croissant – French Butter	8
Double Berry Muffin	13
Lemon Card Box Cake	9
Pain au Raisin	9
Pret Bakewell	9
Yogurt & Pecan Muffin	15

Pret Pots & Desserts

Cherry Breakfast Bowl	10
Choc Bar	16
Chocolate Mousse	13
Dried Mango	6
Honey & Granola Pret Pot	7
Hot & Cold Granola	16
Lemon Cheesecake	11
Love Bar	9
Porridge with Compote	6
Porridge with Honey	7
Pret Bar	7
Pret Caramel	11
Pret Fruit Salad	3
Superfruit Bowl	2
Very Berry Breakfast Bowl	10
Very Berry Pret Pot	4

Crisps & Snacks

Chilli Cashews	13
Chocolate Crackle Topcorn	6
Croxton Manor Cheddar & Red Onion Crisps	5
Double Cheddar & Onion Topcorn	3
Maldon Sea Salt Crisps	5
Parsnip, Beetroot & Carrot Crisps	3
Pretzel	10
Rock Salt Topcorn	3
Savoury Original Topcorn	3
Sea Salt & Organic Cider Vinegar Crisps	5
Spicy Piri Chilli Crisps	5
Sweet Potato & Chipotle Chilli Crisps	4
Yogurt Nuts	12

Breakfast Subs

Bacon	7
Bacon & Egg (includes cheese)	9
Cheese & Egg	10
Mega Breakfast	14
Sausage	10
Sausage & Egg	13

Classic Subs

Chicken & Bacon Ranch	13
Italian B.M.T	12
Meatball Marinara	14
Spicy Italian	14
Steak & Cheese	9
Subway Melt	9
Tuna	11
Veggie Patty	10

Low Fat Subs

Beef	7
Chicken Breast	8
Ham	7
Peri Peri Chicken	8
Subway Club	8
Sweet Onion Chicken Teriyaki	10
Turkey Breast	7
Turkey Breast & Ham	7
Veggie Delite	5

Salads

Beef	3
Chicken Breast	4
Ham	3
Sweet Onion Chicken Teriyaki	5
Turkey Breast & Ham	3
Turkey Breast	3

Snack Menu

All Day Breakfast Mini Wrap	9
Bowl of Meatballs	9
Cheese Toastie	6
Pepperoni Pizza Toastie	7

Treats

Chocolate Chip Candy	6
Sugar Cookie	6
Sugared Donut	6
White Chip Macadamia Nut Cookie	6

Meat Pasties

Cheese & Bacon	25
Chicken & Vegetable	18
Chicken Balti	20
Lamb & Mint	21
Pork & Apple	21
Sausage Roll – Large	10
Steak & Stilton	21
Steak & Tribute	21
Steak – Small	11
Steak – Medium	19
Steak – Large	15
Turkey & Cranberry	20

Fish & Vegetable Pasties

Cheese & Mushroom	22
Cheese & Onion	22
Cheese, Tomato & Basil	21
Deluxe Vegetable	19
Salmon	16
Wholemeal Vegetable	18

All Day Brunch (Grills)

Bacon & Egg in a Bun	8
Bacon in a Bun	5
Classic Bacon Grill or Wimpy All-Day Breakfast	20
Classic Grill	21
Gourmet Platter	16
Sausage, Egg & Chips	17
Steak Platter	20
The International Grill	25
Wimpy Breakfast	12

Burgers

Barbelicious BBQ Burger	18
Bender in a Bun	11
Bender in a Bun with Cheese	12
Classic Bacon Cheeseburger	11
Classic Burger	9
Classic Burger with Cheese	10
Classic Kingsize	15
Chicken & Bacon Melt	12
Chicken Chunks with Chips	21
Chicken in a Bun	11
Gourmet Chicken	13
Halfpounder Burger	23
Hot 'N' Spicy Chicken Fillet in a Bun	12
Megaburger	16
Pork Rib	12
Quarterpounder	15
Quarterpounder with Cheese	16

Jacket Potatoes

Plain with Butter	13
with Baked Beans	16
with Coleslaw or Tuna Mayo	22
with Grated Cheese	27

Alternative Meals

Haddock, Chips & Peas	19
Lemon Pepper Quorn	16
Scampi & Chips	17
Spicy Beanburger	17
Wimpy Club	17

Salads

Fish or Scampi or Spicy Beanburger	11
Gourmet Chicken	6
Hot 'N' Spicy Chicken	8
Steak	9

French

Soupes

Crème Vichyssoise	16
Potage à la Citrouille	3
Soupe à l'Oignon Gratinée	8
Soupe au Pistou	3
Soupe de Légumes	1
Soupe de Moules	7
Soupe de Poisson	4
Velouté Dubarry	9

Entrées

Andouille de Vire ou Guémené	2
Avocat aux Crevettes ou au Crabe	7
Foie Gras	5
Macédoine de Légumes	15
Mousse de Canard	6
Pâté de Foie	5
Quiche	15
Rillettes de Porc	6
Saucisson Sec	5
Soufflé au Fromage	8
Tarte à l'Oignon	10

Plats Principaux / Poissons

Daurade au Vin Blanc	5
Filets de Sole à la Normande	6
Gratin de Fruits de Mer	6
Moules Marinières	9
Pavé de Saumon à l'Oseille	15
Sandre au Four Sauce Béarnaise	12
Thon Rouge en Piperade	11
Truites aux Amandes	15

Plats Principaux / Viandes

Andouillettes Grillées	15
Blanquette de Veau	7
Boulettes de Boeufs	6
Canard aux Navets	13
Confit de Canard ou d'Oie	12
Endives au Jambon Sauce Béchamel	9
Entrecôte Grillée	7
Entrecôte Poivre Vert	9
Hachis Parmentier	12
Lapin de Garenne aux Pruneaux	11
Navarin d'Agneau	18
Poule au Pot	13
Poulet Rôti	6
Tartiflette	12

Snacks Rapides

Brie Baguette	32
Crêpe aux Champignons	25
Croque Madame	32
Croque Monsieur	29
Croquette de Poisson	26
Plateau Brasserie	16
Poulet Baguette	27
Saumon Baguette	30
Steak Baguette	30

Hors D'Oeuvres

Camembert Chaud	21
Champignon Farci	13
Crevettes à l'ail	13
Escargots	9
Gravadlax	6
Pâté de Campagne	10
Petite Friture	14
Soupe à l'Oignon	11

Salades

Chèvre Chaud	20
Niçoise	16
Poulet et Lardons	17

Poissons

Filet de Loup	11
Marmite de Poissons	19
Saumon Grillé	18
Truite aux Amandes	17

Plats Brasserie

Boeuf Bourguignon	24
Confit de Canard	26
Coq au Vin	26
Le Demi Poulet with Garlic Butter	31
Les Moules Bretonne with Frites	22
Les Moules Mariniere with Frites	22
Les Moules Provencale with Frites	20
Tagliatelle aux Champignons	26
Tajine de Legumes	18

Grillades

Chateaubriand	23
Entrecôte	21
Gérard Burger	27
Gérard Burger with Gruyère & Smoked Bacon	33

Gérard Burger with Gruyère, Red Onions & Jalapeño Peppers	30
Le Filet	21
Onglet	25
Poulet Burger	24
Tranche de Gigot	27

Accompagnements

Buttered French Beans	2
Dauphinoise Potatoes	14
French Fries	12
New Potatoes Roasted with Rosemary	7
Toasted Garlic Baguette	4
Toasted Garlic Baguette with Gruyère	9

Desserts

Assiette de Fruits	5
Cheesecake au Café	10
Crème Brûlée	10
Crêpes Suzette	12
Fondant au Chocolat	14
Gauffre Chaude	15
Le Plateau de Fromages	12
Poire Belle Hélène	16
Tarte au Citron	12
Tarte Tatin	11

Casse Croutes

Assiette Campagnard, complete	21
Camembert au Four	14
Fougasse	23
Fougasse Bread & Dips	33
Marinated Mixed Olives	4
Mixed Bread Basket	14
Mixed Nuts	11
Petit Saucisson	7

Hors D'Oeuvres

Asiette de Jambon Cru et Remoulade	8
Beignets de Carbe	6
Escargots	10
Fritôts de Camembert	11
Petite Salade de Chèvre	8
Terrine Maison	7

Sandwiches & Salades

Baguette Poulet	34
Baguette Rouge	40
Croque Monsieur	27
Salade César au Poulet Grillé	13
Salade de Chèvre	14
Salade de Toulouse	24
Salade Paysanne	19
Saumon à la Niçoise	18

Les Grillades & Plats Rapide

Bavette, 8oz	24
Cromesquis de Saumon	16
Entrecote Rouge	29
Minute Steak, 5oz	39
Penne Légumes	16
Quiche Lorraine	26
Steak Frites, 7oz	27
Terrine Maison	7

Speciality de la Maison

Boeuf Bourguignon	21
Confit de Canard	23
Cromesquis d'Eglefin Fumé	16
Demi Poulet	41
Moules – Classic Café Rouge Mussels	5
Saucisse de Toulouse	23
Sole-Limande	12
Tarte aux Epinards	12

Italian

Soups & Starters

Anchovy Fillets in Green Sauce	9
Baked Mussels	2
Cream of Asparagus Soup	6
Cream of Porcini Soup	14
Fish Soup	6
Gazpacho	6
Genoese Pesto Minestrone	10
Milanese Minestrone	4
Seasonal Minestrone	9
Tomato Bruschetta	6

Risotto

Asparagus	15
Mushroom	15
Seafood	16
Wine & Mushroom	15

Pasta

Farfalle with Smoked Pancetta	20
Fusilli with Mushrooms	13
Lasagne alla Bolognese	23
Lasagne Napoletana	18
Macaroni au Gratin	17
Orecchiette with Tomato & Ricotta	11
Penne Arrabiata	15
Potato Gnocchi with Tomato Sauce	13
Ravioli Napoletana	12
Rigatoni with Meatballs	17
Spaghetti alla Carbonara	17
Spaghetti Amatriciana	12
Spaghetti with Tuna	12
Tagliatelle with Cream, Peas & Ham	15
Tagliatelle with Mushrooms	17
Trofie with Pesto Sauce	20

Pasta Sauces

Bolognese	11
Pesto	7
Seafood	7
Tomato	2

Desserts

Biscotti alla Cannella	10
Coffee Baba	10
Tiramisu	20
Zabaglione	13

Antipasti

Antipasti Selezione (Half)	**19**
Bruschetta	**7**
Calamari	**15**
Capra Grill	**10**
Cod & Pancetta Fishcake	**11**
Garlic Bread	**6**
Garlic Bread with Cheese	**9**
Insalata Pomodoro e Pesto	**7**
Marinated Olives	**5**
Mushrooms al Forno	**8**
Prawns al Piccante	**9**
Prosciutto & Mozzarella Crostini	**9**
Warm Spinach & Mushroom Dip	**10**

Insalata

Chef's Salad	**14**
Chicken Caesar Salad	**14**
Filetto di Salmone all'Insalata	**8**
Insalata di Pollo e Pancetta	**14**
Insalata Tricolore	**15**
King Prawn al Limone Piccante	**12**

Pasta

Fusilli alla Cacciatora	**17**
Lasagne	**17**
Linguine Gamberi e Rucola	**15**
Penne al Pollo della Casa	**27**
Penne del Giardino	**17**
Penne e Pollo Pomodorini Basilico	**14**
Penne Paesana	**21**
Polpette al Forno	**20**
Ravioli ai Funghi e Ricotta	**25**
Ravioli Burro e Pesce	**21**
Rigatoni e Polpette	**20**
Spaghetti al Pomodoro	**12**
Spaghetti alla Bolognese	**20**
Spaghetti Carbonara	**22**

Mains

Ciabatta al Petto di Pollo	**26**
Pollo Marsala	**18**
Risotto Frutti di Mare	**21**
Risotto Pollo e Funghi	**25**
Risotto Vegetariana	**20**
Salmone Rustico	**22**
Terrina Mediterranea	**19**
The ASK Burger	**38**

Pizza & Calzone

Calzone con Carne Piccante	29
Calzone con Funghi e Formaggio	30
Calzone di Pollo e Pancetta	27
Estiva	23
Fiorentina	23
Four Seasons	26
Margherita	18
Napoletana	24
Pollo Piccante	24
Stromboli	23
Tropicale	20
Vegetariana	23
Vesuvio	23

Sides

Caesar Salad	5
Ciabatta Bread	10
Green Beans (with Butter)	2
Mixed Salad (with Dressing)	2
Roasted New Charlotte Potatoes	8
Rocket Salad (with Dressing)	2
Seasoned Chips	14

Dessert

Apple Rustica	21
Banoffee Pie	12
Chocolate Cake	18
Gelati, per Scoop	6
Honeycomb Cheesecake	14
Lemon Tart	11
Our Chocolate Nemesis	20
Profiteroles al Cioccolato	14
Sorbetti, 2 Scoops	4
Tiramisu	11

Antipasti

Antipasto Misto	17
Bruschetta	5
Formaggio Fritto	9
Funghi Arrosto	13
Gamberi	9
Mozzarella e Pomodoro	7

Side Orders

Ciabatta	12
Diced Herb Potatoes	5
Garlic Grossini	7
Garlic Grossini with Cheese	10
Insalata Mista (with Dressing)	1
Insalata Rucola (with Dressing & Parmesan)	3
Olive Marinate	4
Pane Bella	11
Roasted New Potatoes	4

Insalata & Panini

Panino Pesto Rosso	14
Panino Pollo	22
Pollo Cesare	15
Pollo e Pancetta Salad	13
Tonno Salad	9

Pizzeria

Carne Mista	29
Margherita	20
Pepperoni	26
Pesto Rosso e Legumi	26
Pollo Piccantina	23
Quattro Stagioni	27
Salmone e Asparagi	26
Speck e Rucola	25

Carne, Pollo & Pesce

Burger Italiano	26
Burger Italiano with Bacon	29
Burger Italiano with Smoked Mozzarella	28
Controfiletto ai Ferri	16
Crocchette di Pesce	13
Pollo alla Griglia with Roasted Vegetables & New Potatoes	15
Pollo alla Griglia with Salad & Fries	21
Pollo Cacciatore	18
Salmone al Pomodoro	12

Pasta & Al Forno

Fusilli Pollo Spinaci	**19**
Fusilli Pomodorini	**15**
Penne Marco Polo	**17**
Penne Zafferano	**19**
Polpette Americano	**17**
Spaghetti Bolognese	**15**
Spaghetti Carbonara	**20**
Spaghetti Gamberi	**16**
Spaghetti Genovese	**17**

Dolci

Banoffee Italiano	**13**
Berry Tiramisu	**12**
Cioccolato Napoletano	**17**
Fondente al Cioccolato	**20**
Gelati	**12**
Mascarpone Cheesecake	**11**
Sorbetti	**3**
The Godfather	**28**
The Godfather with a Full Measure of Amaretto	**30**
Tiramisu	**11**
Torta Limone	**11**

Starters & Sides

BBQ Dip	1
BBQ Ribs	3
Chicken Kickers	10
Chicken Strippers	12
Chicken Wings Lightly Spiced	12
Coleslaw	5
Garlic & Herb Dip	6
Garlic Pizza Bread	7
Honey & Mustard Dip	4
Potato Wedges	4
Sweet Chilli Dip	2

Medium Regular Crust (Per Slice)

American Hot or Big Smokey	5
Americano	7
Bacon Double Cheese	6
Cheese & Tomato	4
Chicken Feast or Chicken Tikka	5
Extravaganza or Full House	6
Ham & Pineapple	5
Hot & Spicy	5
Meat Lovers	6
Meatball Mayhem or Meateor	7
Meltdown – The Revenge	5
Mighty Meaty or Pepperoni Passion	6
Piri Piri	4
Tandoori Hot or Texas BBQ	5
The Sizzler	7
Veg-A-Roma	6
Vegetarian Supreme or Vegi Volcano	5

Medium Double Decadence (Per Slice)

American Hot or Big Smokey	8
Americano	9
Cheese & Tomato	7
Chicken Feast	6
Extravaganza or Full House	9
Ham & Pineapple	8
Hot & Spicy	8
Meat Lovers	9
Meatball Mayhem or Meateor	10
Mighty Meaty or Pepperoni Passion	9
Tandoori Hot or Texas BBQ	8
The Sizzler	9
Vegetarian Supreme	7
Vegi Volcano	8

Breads & Nibbles

Garlic Pizza Bread with Mozzarella	14
Garlic Pizza Bread with Rosemary & Sea Salt	10
Garlic Pizza Bread with Tomato & Basil	9
Marinated Olives	7
Raisin Bread Brushetta with Tomatoes, Basil, Garlic & Red Onion	7
Roasted Almonds with Smoked Paprika (Half)	6
Selection of Italian Breads with Olive Oil (Half)	14

Starters

Beef Carpaccio with Balsamic & Sundried Tomato Dressing	9
Calamari Deep Fried with Lemon Mayonnaise	14
Chicken Skewers with Pancetta & Mozzarella	15
Field Mushrooms with Tuscan Ham & Mozzarella	14
Fresh Figs, Tuscan Ham & Mozzarella with Dressing	9
Fritto Misto	18
Goat's Cheese, Beetroot & Balsamic Puff Pastry Tart	15
Mussels in White Wine & Cream with Ciabatta	19
Red Pepper & Vine Tomato Soup with Mascarpone	9
Tiger Prawns in a Garlic, Tomato & Cream Sauce	16
Warm Figs, Walnut & Goat's Cheese Raisin Bread Bruschetta	19

Salads

Apple, Gorgonzola, Walnut, Baby Gem & Spinach	17
Flaked Hot Smoked Salmon	17
Grilled Chicken Caesar	19
Warm Goat's Cheese & Raisin Bread Bruscetta with Mixed Greens	22
Warm Shredded Duck with Crisp Pancetta & Asparagus	18

Pasta & Risotto

Chicken Primavera	36
Italian Meatballs in a Tomato Sauce on Spaghetti	26
Linguini Garlic Prawns with Tomato, Chilli & Rocket	19
Lobster & Prawn Linguine	17
Oven Baked Homemade Lasagne	24
Penne Arrabiata with Tomato & Chilli	16
Penne Arrabiata with Pepperoni	26
Penne with Salmon, Peas & Spinach in Cream Sauce	27
Spaghetti Bolognese	16
Spaghetti Carbonara	24
Spaghetti Tossed in a Light Tomato Ragu & Basil	16
Spaghetti with Chicken, Pesto, Green Beans & Sun Dried Tomatoes	21
Tiger Prawn, Mussels & Calamari Risotto	24
Vegetarian Primavera	32
Wild Mushroom Risotto	21
Wild Mushroom Risotto with Italian Smoked Bacon	26

Seafood

Fillets of Dorada with Sundried Tomato Oil & Lemon Risotto	22
Grilled Salmon with Pesto Mash & Lemon Butter Jus	30
Half Grilled Lobster with Fries & Thermadore Sauce	27
Roasted Cod on Pepperoni & Tomato Puy Lentils	18
Salt Baked Seabass with Orange & Fennel	13
Seared Sashimi Tuna with Rocket & Chilled Coriander Salsa	12

Meat

Chargrilled Chicken Breast with Lentils & Green Beans	16
Chargrilled Lamb Cutlets with Peas & a Red Wine Jus	26
Duck Breast with Leek, Carrot & Pancetta Bound with Cream	27
Italian Beefburger with Smoked Provola Cheese & Fries	38
Pork Cutlet Saltimbocca alla Romana with Cured Tuscan Ham & Sage served with Rosemary Potatoes	28
Roasted Chicken Breast wrapped in Proscuitto served on Green Pesto, Rocket & Goat's Cheese Risotto	24
Suckling Pig with Cream & Butter Mash & Apple Sauce	28

28 Day Aged Premium Steak

6oz Pan Fried Fillet with Wild Mushrooms, Cipollini Onions & Valpolicella Reduction	15
8oz Sirloin infused with Garlic, Rosemary & Green Peppercorns	15
10oz Rib-eye Chargrilled with Asparagus, Parmesan & Truffle Oil	30
10oz Fillet Chargrilled with Grilled Tomato & Fries	31
Rump Steak with Garlic, Chilli, Peppercorn, Sea Salt & Rocket	16

Side Orders

Baked Rosemary & Garlic Roast Potatoes	9
Cream & Butter Mash	12
French Beans with Shallots (with Butter)	3
Fries	12
Garlic Mushrooms	4
Italian Fried Courgette	4
Panache of Mixed Vegetables	3
Steamed Spinach with Sea Salt (with Butter)	3
Sugar Snap Peas (with Butter)	3

Desserts

Affogato	11
Banoffi Pie	26
Chocolate & Orange Mousse	16
Italian Cheeseboard	20
Lemon Sorbet	4
Nutella & Mascarpone Calzone	24
Sticky Toffee Pudding	18
Tiramisu	17
Three Scoop Ice Cream Coupe with Almond Flakes	19
Warm Pear & Almond Tart with Vanilla Ice Cream	26

Intros

Noci	9
Olives Marinate	4
Rustica Tomatoes	2

Starters & Sides

Antipasto Platter for 2 (per person)	13
Arancini	10
Baked Dough Balls & Garlic Butter	10
Baked Dough Balls (no Garlic Butter)	6
Bruschetta	13
Bruschetta con Funghi	15
Ciabatta Bread (2 Slices)	2
Dough Sticks	6
Formaggio Bread	9
Garlic Bread	7
Garlic Bread with Mozzarella	8
Porcini Mushroom Risotto	12
Risotto Primavera	11
Rocket & Pecorino Salad	4

Classic Pizza

American	22
American Hot	22
Capricciosa	23
Diavolo	22
Fiorentina	22
Four Seasons	18
Funghi di Bosco	20
Giardineria	26
Il Padrino	25
La Reine	20
Margherita	18
Padana	22
Pollo ad Astra	18
Quattro Formaggi	20
Siciliana	23
Sloppy Giuseppe	21
Soho	21
Veneziana	20
Zucchine Funghi	20

Leggera Menu

Insalata Verde (no Dressing)	0
Crostini al Pomodoro	5
Margherita	13
Gustosa	14
Mare e Monti	14

	ProPoints value
Verdure	16
Sotto Zero	5

Romana Pizza

Al Tirolo	24
American or American Hot	24
Campo di Fiori	26
Capricciosa	24
Diavolo	24
Etna	31
Fiorentina	24
Four Seasons	20
Funghi di Bosco	20
Giardineria	27
Il Padrino	27
La Reine	22
Margherita	20
Padana	23
Pollo ad Astra	23
Pollo Pancetta	25
Quattro Formaggi	24
Salsiccia	29
Siciliana	25
Sloppy Giuseppe	22
Soho	23
Veneziana	22
Zucchine Funghi	22

Theo Randall's Pizza

Theo's Favorita	19
Theo's Favorita Vegetarian	21
Theo's Gamberettini	23

Pasta

Cannelloni	19
Lasagne Classico	19
Melanzane Parmagiana	18
Pollo Pesto	27

Salads & Dressings

Balsamic Dressing	2
Bosco Salad, no Dressing, no Dough Sticks	14
Bosco Salad with Dough Sticks & Dressing	23
Bosco Salad with Dough Sticks, no Dressing	20
Caesar Dressing	4
Caesar Salad – Light Dressing	7
Caesar Salad – no Dressing	5
Caesar Salad with House Dressing	9
Grand Chicken Caesar Salad, no Dressing, no Dough Sticks	9
Grand Chicken Caesar Salad with Dough Sticks & Dressing	20

Grand Chicken Caesar Salad with Dough Sticks, no Dressing	16
Grand Chicken Caesar Salad with Dressing, no Dough Sticks	13
Honey & Mustard Dressing	2
House Dressing	1
Light Dressing	1
Mixed Side Salad - House Dressing	4
Mixed Side Salad - Light Dressing	3
Mixed Side Salad - no Dressing	0
Mozzarella & Tomato Salad	13
Mozzarella & Tomato Salad - no Oil	11
Niçoise Salad with Dough Sticks & Dressing	20
Niçoise Salad with Dough Sticks, no Dressing	17
Niçoise Salad with Dough Sticks, Light Dressing	19
Nostrana Salad, no Dressing, no Dough Sticks	13
Nostrana Salad with Dough Sticks & Dressing	23
Nostrana Salad with Dough Sticks, no Dressing	19
Nostrana Salad with Dressing, no Dough Sticks	16
Nostrana with Light Dressing	22
Pollo Salad with Dough Sticks & Dressing	18
Pollo Salad with Dough Sticks, no Dressing	14
Pollo Salad with Dressing, no Dough Sticks	11
Pollo Salad, no Dressing, no Dough Sticks	8
Pollo Salad with Light Dressing	17
Pollo Verdure Salad, no Dough Sticks, no Dressing	3
Pollo Verdure Salad with Dough Sticks & Dressing	13
Pollo Verdure Salad with Dough Sticks, no Dressing	10
Pollo Verdure Salad with Dressing, no Dough Sticks	6

Desserts

Banoffee Pie	11
Banoffee Pie with Cream	17
Banoffee Pie with Ice Cream or Marscarpone	14
Caffé Merenghina	4
Caffé Reale	6
Cheesecake	11
Cheesecake with Cream	15
Cheesecake with Ice Cream or Marscarpone	14
Chocolate Fudge Cake	10
Chocolate Fudge Cake with Cream	14
Chocolate Fudge Cake with Ice Cream or Marscarpone	13
Chocolate Glory	19
Chocolate Straw	1
Coppa Gelato – All Flavours - one scoop	3
Cream Portion	4
Lemon Gelato with Chocolate Straw	6
Lemon Tart	13
Mascarpone	4
Semi Freddo Reale	5
Tiramisu	14
Toffee Fudge Glory	19
Trio of Profiteroles	12

Starters & Sides

3 Cheese Melt	**13**
BBQ Chicken Wings	**11**
Breaded Chicken Strips	**8**
Bruschetta	**10**
Cheesy Jalepeño Poppers	**11**
Cheese Nachos, to share (Total Dish)	**19**
Chicken Caesar Salad	**8**
Chicken Caesar Salad, Small	**7**
Chilli Nachos	**16**
Chilli Onion Rings	**5**
Classic Caesar Salad, Small	**5**
Garlic Bread	**10**
Garlic Bread with Cheese	**15**
Garlic Ciabatta	**11**
Garlic Mushrooms	**15**
Hot 'n' Kicking Chicken Strips	**7**
Margherita Tortizza	**14**
Mixed Olives	**4**
Mozzarella & Tomato Salad	**10**
Potato Wedges	**10**
Prawn Caesar Salad, Small	**6**
Savoury Seasoned Fries	**7**
Texan BBQ Chicken Wings	**9**
Tuscani Platter, to share (Half)	**16**

Cheesy Bites Pizza (Per Slice)

BBQ Deluxe	**10**
Chicken Supreme	**9**
Farmhouse	**9**
Hawaiian	**9**
Hot 'N' Spicy	**9**
Margherita	**9**
Meat Feast	**11**
Meaty BBQ	**8**
Pepperoni Feast	**11**
Seafood Lovers	**9**
Super Supreme	**11**
Supreme	**9**
The Sizzler – Cajun Chicken or Spicy Beef	**8**
The Sizzler – Spicy Mushroom	**7**
Vegetable Supreme	**9**
Vegetarian Hot One	**9**

Medium Italian Pizza (Per Slice)

BBQ Deluxe	**7**
Chicken Supreme	**6**
Farmhouse	**5**
Hawaiian	**6**

Hot 'N' Spicy	6
Margherita	6
Meat Feast	7
Meaty BBQ	4
Pepperoni Feast	7
Seafood Lovers	6
Super Supreme	8
Supreme	7
The Sizzler – Cajun Chicken or Spicy Mushroom	4
The Sizzler – Spicy Beef	5
Vegetable Supreme	6
Vegetarian Hot One	5

Medium Pan Pizza (Per Slice)

BBQ Deluxe	7
Chicken Supreme	7
Farmhouse	7
Hawaiian	7
Hot 'N' Spicy	7
Margherita	7
Meat Feast	8
Meaty BBQ	6
Pepperoni Feast	8
Seafood Lovers	7
Super Supreme	9
Supreme	9
The Sizzler – Cajun Chicken	5
The Sizzler – Spicy Beef	5
The Sizzler – Spicy Mushroom	5
Vegetable Supreme	7
Vegetarian Hot One	7

Stuffed Crust Pizza (Per Slice)

BBQ Deluxe	10
Chicken Supreme	10
Farmhouse	8
Hawaiian	9
Hot 'N' Spicy	9
Margherita	9
Meat Feast	11
Meaty BBQ	7
Pepperoni Feast	11
Seafood Lovers	9
Super Supreme	11
Supreme	10
The Sizzler – Cajun Chicken or Spicy Beef	8
The Sizzler – Spicy Mushroom	7
Vegetable Supreme	9
Vegetarian Hot One	10

Tuscani Pizzas (Unsliced)

Caprina	26
Chicken & Mushroom	28
Mediterranean Meats	28
Rocket & Proscuitto	22
Verde	24

Pasta & Main Salads

4 Cheese Pasta	17
Alfredo Pasta	14
Arrabiata Pasta	12
Bolognese Pasta	13
Chicken & Mushroom Pasta Bake	12
Chicken Alfredo Pasta	15
Chicken Caesar Salad with Bacon	15
House Chicken Salad	11
Prawn Caesar Salad	12
Salmon Pasta Bake	19
Spinach & Ricotta Cannelloni	15
Tagliatelle alla Carbonara	15
Tomato & Mozzerella Mezzaluna	9
Tori's Tomato Pasta Bake	12
Traditional Lasagne	16

Salad Station (Per Spoonful)

Apple & Grape Mix	0
Baby Potatoes	2
Bacon Bits	14
Beetroot & Carrot with Balsamic Vinegrette	1
Breadsticks	10
Coleslaw	5
Cous Cous	6
Dried Fruit Mix	7
Gemelli Pasta	4
Grated Hard Cheese, 100g	11
Large Salad Croutons, 100g	13
Melon Pieces	0
Potato Salad	4
Sunflower Seeds, 1 tablespoon	3
Sweetcorn	2
Tomato Pasta Salad	5
Tortilla Chips	14

Dips & Dressings

1000 Island	2
BBQ Sauce	1
Blue Cheese	7
Caesar Dressing	2

Extra Virgin Olive Oil with Balsamic Vinegar	3
Extra Virgin Olive Oil with Italian Herbs	4
Garlic & Chilli Dipping Oil	6
Garlic & Herb Dip	3
Houmous	7
Lemon Infused Oil	6
Low Fat Vinaigrette	2
Mayonnaise Light	5
Salsa	4
Sweet Chilli Sauce	1
Tomato Ketchup	1

Desserts

Banoffee Pie	10
Chocolate Cheesecake	6
Chocolate Fudge Cake	19
Chocolate Raisins	11
Clotted Cream Cheesecake	6
Coated Chocolate Beans	13
Cookie Dough	27
Festive Fruit Meltdown	18
Ice Cream Mix	4
Lemon & Ginger Cheesecake	6
Profiteroles	11
Strawberry Cheescake	10
Tiramisu	7
Toffee Apple Meltdown	23
Traditional Ice Cream	7

Bread and Olives

Dough Sticks	6
Garlic Bread	17
Garlic Bread with Cheese	21
Goddess Olives	4
Italian Bread Board	14
Mixed Olives	3
Tomato Pesto Bread	16

Antipasti

Angelo's Mussels	7
Antipasto Siciliano	10
Antipasto Zizzi, to share (Half)	18
Arancini	22
Bruschetta al Pomodoro	8
Calamari	10
Crostini Formaggio di Capra	12
Tricolore	6

Insalate

Ciabatta Pollo	21
Insalata Boccincini	15
Insalata Cacciatore	20
Insalata Cesare	13
Insalata Mista (with Dressing)	5
Insalata Nizza	11
Insalata Rucola (with Dressing & Cheese)	9
Insalate Spinaci e Pancetta	11

Pasta

Casareccia Pollo Piccante	16
Fettucine alla Carbonara	24
Linguine Gamberi	16
Ravioli di Capra	19
Rigatoni con Pollo e Funghi	14
Spaghetti alla Bolognese	20
Spaghetti Polpette	23
Spaghetti Pomodoro	16
Strozzapreti Pesto Rosso	17

Risotto

Risotto al Funghi con Pollo	22
Risotto di Pesce	21
Risotto Verde	18

Pizza

Diavola	27
Fiorentina	28

ProPoints value

Funghi	22
Margherita	22
Pollo al Rosmarino	28
Quattro Formaggi	30
Quattro Stagioni	28
Sofia	34
Trentino	25

Rustica

Bufala	24
Capricciosa	30
Mare e Monti	31
Mezzo e Mezzo	27
Piccante	35
Primavera	28

Calzone

Carne Piccante	41
Clarissa	33
Stromboli	29

Al Forno

Aubergine Parmigiana	15
Lasagne al Forno	23
Penne della Casa	31

Carne e Pesce

Calamari	13
Fine Green Beans	0
Pollo con Pesto	19
Roasted Vegetables	4
Salmon Salsa Verde	17
Sea Bass al Vino	13
Tuscan Potatoes	6
Zizzi Sirloin Steak	19

Desserts

Chocolate Melt	18
Gelati e Sorbetti (2 Scoops of Ice Cream)	3
Mela Croccante	11
Pannacotta	16
Torta Amaretti	14
Torta Cioccolata	20
Torta Estiva	14
Torta Limone	12
Tiramisu	15
Zabaione	10

Pubs & Carveries

Starters

Beefeater Combo, to share (Half)	17
Chicken Tikka Skewers	6
Dipping Bread Trio, to share (Half)	17
Duck & Port Pâté with Brown or White Toast	13
Garlic & Herb Breaded Mushrooms	15
Honeydew Melon	0
Koftas	9
Mushroom Tart Tatin	16
Nachos, to share (Half)	15
Potato Shells with Melted Cheddar Cheese & Bacon	17
Potato Shells with Melted Cheddar Cheese & Spiced Onion Marmalade	14
Prawn Cocktail with Malted or White Bread	11
Prawn Trio	15
Whitebait	16

Bar Meals – Sandwiches & Jackets

Brie with Cranberry Sauce, Malted or White Baguette	18
Cheddar Cheese & Spiced Onion Marmalade, Malted Baguette	23
Cheddar Cheese & Spiced Onion Marmalade, White Baguette	24
Chicken Caesar, Malted or White Baguette	17
Chicken Mayonnaise Salad, Malted or White Baguette	16
Classic Club Sandwich on Malted Bread	30
Classic Club Sandwich on White Bread	28
Hot Sausage & Spiced Onion Marmalade, Malted Baguette	29
Hot Sausage & Spiced Onion Marmalade, White Baguette	30
Jacket Potato with Cheddar Cheese & Baked Beans	17
Jacket Potato with Cheddar Cheese, Baked Beans & Bacon	19
Jacket Potato with Chilli & Cheese	21
Jacket Potato with Tuna Mayonnaise	14
Prawns in Marie Rose Sauce, Malted Baguette	13
Prawns in Marie Rose Sauce, White Baguette	14
Steak Club Sandwich on Malted Bread	19
Steak Club Sandwich on White Bread	18
Tuna Mayonnaise, Malted Baguette	15
Tuna Mayonnaise, White Baguette	16

Bar Meals – Classic Favourites, Chargrills & Tempting Extras

Beef & Ale Pie	39
Chicken Burger with Cheese & Bacon	35
Chilli con Carne	21
Chips	13
Gammon Steak & Egg	18
Paprika Chicken Burger with Mayonnaise or Sour Cream	14
Potato Shells with Cheese & Onion	28
Sausage & Mash	29

| Smoked Paprika Chicken Burger with Mayonnaise or Sour Cream | 27 |
| Tortilla Chips | 7 |

Ultimate Chargrills

6oz Beef Burger with Chargrilled Red Pepper & Cheddar Cheese	36
6oz Beef Burger with Cheddar Cheese & Bacon	38
6oz Beef Burger with Flat Mushroom & Black & Blue Sauce	35
7oz Fillet Steak with Chips	20
7oz Rump Steak with Chips	18
8oz Sirloin Steak with Chips	22
9oz Beef Burger with Chargrilled Red Pepper & Cheddar Cheese	39
9oz Beef Burger with Cheddar Cheese & Bacon	39
9oz Beef Burger with Flat Mushroom & Black & Blue Sauce	38
10oz Rib Eye Steak with Chips	25
British Rib Eye on the Bone	23
Fisherman's Chargrilled Selection	16
Giant Chicken Skewer	27
Rack of Ribs with Bourbon & Black BBQ Sauce	37
Rack of Ribs with Spiced Worcestershire Sauce	35
Rack of Ribs with Sticky Tomato & Chilli Sauce	37
Thick-Cut Sirloin	20

Meat, Fish & Vegetarian

Chargrilled Chicken	8
Chicken Breast & Maple Pork Ribs	21
Chicken Breast Wrapped in Bacon	12
Chicken Tikka Skewers	14
Double Gammon Steak & Egg	22
Double Gammon Steak & Pineapple	23
Fish & Chips	27
Garlic & Herb Chicken	23
Half a Rack of Ribs	16
Maple Pork Ribs	23
Minted Loin of Lamb	11
Mixed Grill	19
Mushroom Tart Tatin	15
Plain Chicken	21
Quesadilla Wrap	26
Rack of Lamb	13
Salmon Fillet	16
Salmon Fillet with Béarnaise Sauce	22
Sea Bass Fillets	10
Smoked Paprika Chicken	9

Pasta & Salads

Caesar Salad	12
Caesar Salad with Bacon & Stilton	24
Caesar Salad with Chargrilled Chicken Breast	16
Caesar Salad with Salmon Fillet	22

Caesar Salad with Skewered Prawns	15
Chimi Churi Spiral Pasta	21
Chimi Churi Spiral Pasta with Chicken Breast	25
Chimi Churi Spiral Pasta with Salmon Fillet	31
Creamy Pesto Spiral Pasta	18
Creamy Pesto Spiral Pasta with Chicken Breast	22
Creamy Pesto Spiral Pasta with Salmon Fillet	27
House Salad	3
House Salad with Bacon & Stilton	15
House Salad with Chargrilled Chicken Breast	7
House Salad with Salmon Fillet	13
House Salad with Skewered Prawns	6
Mediterranean Spiral Pasta	16
Mediterranean Spiral Pasta with Chicken Breast	20
Mediterranean Spiral Pasta with Salmon Fillet	26
Mediterranean Tomato Risotto	11
Mediterranean Tomato Risotto with Chicken Breast	15
Mediterranean Tomato Risotto with Prawn Skewers	14
Mediterranean Tomato Risotto with Salmon Fillet	21
Pine Nut Salad	6
Pine Nut Salad with Bacon & Stilton	18
Pine Nut Salad with Chargrilled Chicken Breast	10
Pine Nut Salad with Salmon Fillet	16
Pine Nut Salad with Skewered Prawns	8

Great with your Meal

Beefeater Coleslaw	10
Beefeater Grill Extra, to share (Half)	8
Beefeater Spiral Onion Loaf	6
Buttered Mushrooms	5
Buttered New Potatoes	5
Cheddar & Mozzarella Garlic Bread 2 slices	8
Cheddar & Mozzarella Garlic Bread 4 slices	15
Corn on the Cob	9
Dauphinoise Potatoes	16
Extra Chips	13
Fresh Vegetables	2
Garlic Bread	4
Half a Grilled Tomato & a Flat Mushroom	2
Jacket Potato with Butter	12
Mixed Salad Bowl (with Dressing)	1
Onion Ring Tower, to share (Half)	7
Pine Nut Side Salad	3
Piri Piri Rice	7
Side Salad (with Dressing)	1
Spiral Onion Loaf, to share (Half)	7
Stilton & Bacon Side Salad	7
White & Wild Rice	8
Whole Onion Rings	7

Make it Personal

Béarnaise Sauce	2
Black & Blue Sauce	3
Bourbon & Black BBQ Sauce	2
Chimi Churi Sauce (3 tablespoons)	5
Peppercorn & Brandy Sauce	2
Spiced Worcestershire Sauce	4
Sticky Tomato & Chilli Sauce	4

Sunday Roast

Roast Leg of Lamb with Mint Sauce	20
Roast Leg of Lamb with Mint Sauce – Go Large	29
Half a Roast Chicken	26
Roast Topside of British Beef with Horseradish Sauce	17
Roast Topside of British Beef with Horseradish Sauce – Go Large	26

Desserts

Banoffee Pie	19
Belgian Waffle with Chocolate Flavour Fudge Sauce	24
Belgian Waffle with Raspberry Sauce	22
Belgian Waffle with Red Berries	21
Belgian Waffle with Toffee Sauce	23
Brandy Snap Fruit Basket	10
Caramel Apple Crumble Pie with Crème Fraîche	18
Caramel Apple Crumble Pie with Custard	16
Caramel Apple Crumble Pie with Ice Cream	20
Cheese Platter	21
Chocolate Fudge Brownie Sundae	18
Chocolate Layer Cake with Cream or Crème Fraîche	20
Chocolate Layer Cake with Ice Cream	21
Clotted Cream Cheesecake	13
Ice Cream Fruit Sundae	8
Ice Cream topped with Chocolate Sauce	9
Ice Cream topped with Fruit Sauce	7
Profiteroles with Crème Fraîche	16
Profiteroles with Ice Cream	18
Sharing Chocolate Fudge Brownie Sundae (Half)	18
Sharing Profiteroles with Crème Fraîche (Half)	16
Sharing Profiteroles with Ice Cream (Half)	18
Treacle Sponge Pudding with Cream or Crème Fraîche	19
Treacle Sponge Pudding with Custard	18
Treacle Sponge Pudding with Ice Cream	21

Starters

Breaded Camembert Bites	13
Chicken Liver Pâté	15
Combo Feast for 2 (Half)	19
Crispy Fried Whitebait	16
Garlic & Herb Breaded Mushrooms	13
Lamb & Mutton Kebabs	8
Prawn Cocktail	12
Seeded Chicken Goujons	13

Grills

BBQ Ribs	35
Beef Burger	34
Beef Burger with Cheese & Bacon	38
Chicken Burger	19
Chicken Burger with Cheese & Bacon	32
Double Beef Burger	45
Double Beef Burger with Cheese & Bacon	48
Grilled Chicken & BBQ Ribs	28
Grilled Gammon Steak with Eggs	24
Grilled Gammon Steak with One Egg & One Pineapple Slice	22
Grilled Gammon Steak with Pineapple	21
Mixed Grill	38
Rump Steak	21
Sirloin Steak	23
Surf, Turf & Chicken with Peas or Salad	24

Pub Classics

Beef & Ale Pie	36
Beef Lasagne	19
Cheese & Onion Pasty	31
Chicken Tikka Masala	23
Chilli con Carne	18
Cornish Pasty	36
Cottage Pie	15
Grilled Chicken & Bacon Salad	11
Ham, Eggs & Chips	20
Liver & Onions	18
Liver & Onions in a Giant Yorkshire Pudding	30
Minted Lamb Loin	18
Oven Roast Chicken & BBQ Sauce & Jacket Potato	30
Oven Roast Chicken & BBQ Sauce & Chips	33
Oven Roast Chicken & Gravy	28
Sausage & Mash	31
Sausage & Mash in a Giant Yorkshire Pudding	43
Slow Cooked Ham Hock in Parsley Sauce	23
Smothered Chicken	30
Tandoori Vegetable Masala	22
Thai Green Chicken Curry	18
Tomato & Roast Vegetable Pasta	20

Fish

Atlantic Salmon Fillet	**19**
Breaded Wholetail Scampi with Mushy Peas	**34**
Breaded Wholetail Scampi with Peas	**32**
Fisherman's Pie	**20**
Hand Battered Fish & Chips with Mushy Peas	**49**
Hand Battered Fish & Chips with Peas	**48**

Sunday Roast

Mega Roast Beef	**30**
Mega Roast Lamb	**33**
Roast Beef	**19**
Roast Lamb	**22**
Roast Vegetable Wellington	**30**

Side Dishes

Baguette & Butter	**13**
Battered Whole Onion Rings	**5**
Bowl of Chips	**17**
Extra Feast	**13**
Garlic Ciabatta	**4**
Garlic Ciabatta with Melted Cheddar Cheese	**8**
Mixed Side Salad (with Dressing)	**2**
Mushrooms Pan-Fried in Butter	**4**

Passionate about Puddings

Bread & Butter Pudding	**16**
Caramel Apple Crumble	**14**
Caramel Apple Crumble with Cream	**20**
Caramel Apple Crumble with Custard	**16**
Caramel Apple Crumble with Ice Cream	**17**
Chocolate Fudge Cake	**10**
Chocolate Fudge Cake with Cream	**16**
Chocolate Fudge Cake with Ice Cream	**13**
Chocolate Indulgence	**22**
Clotted Cream Cheesecake	**17**
Fresh Fruit Salad	**3**
Fresh Fruit Salad with Cream	**9**
Fresh Fruit Salad with Ice Cream	**6**
Profiteroles	**18**
Sticky Toffee Pudding	**20**
Sticky Toffee Pudding with Cream	**26**
Sticky Toffee Pudding with Custard	**22**
Sticky Toffee Pudding with Ice Cream	**23**
Strawberry Sundae	**15**
Tiramisu	**8**
Ultimate Sharing Sundae for 2 (Half)	**24**

Sharers

Antipasti Platter (Half)	9
Meze Platter (Half)	9
Seafood Platter (Half)	14

Starters

Chicken Liver & Pancetta Pâté	7
Classic Prawn Cocktail	15
Goat's Cheese & Beetroot Fondue	8
Grilled Flat Field Mushrooms	10
Poached Scottish Salmon	7
Spicy Aromatic Farm Assured Chicken	7

Salads & Vegetarian

Aubergine Cannelloni	16
Roasted Vegetable Tagliatelle	12
Wensleydale, Cauliflower & Red Onion Pie	13

Sunday Roast

Roast Topside of Beef	35
Roasted Half Chicken	40
Wensleydale, Cauliflower & Red Onion Pie	25

Fish

Fish Pie	28
Grilled Red Snapper	9
Poached Scottish Salmon	13
Sea Bass Fillet	10

Chicken

Chicken Breast filled with Mozzarella, wrapped in Bacon	17
Lemon & Garlic Marinated Chicken Skewers	15
Spicy Roast Half Chicken	42

Pub Classics

6oz Beef Burger	30
British Beef & Bombardier Ale Pie	27
Free Range Extra Thick Pork Chop	20
Free Range Pork Sausages	22
Hand Carved Honey Roast Ham	28
Lamb Suet Pudding	22
Southern Indian Spiced Lamb Shank Curry	19
Traditional Beer Battered Fish	30
Whitby Scampi	23

Sides

Bowl of Chips	12
Garlic Bread	6
Garlic Bread with Cheese	9
Onion Rings	8
Sautéed Flat Mushrooms	3
Seasonal Vegetables (no Butter)	0
Side Salad (no Dressing)	0

Steak with Chips

7oz Fillet Steak	22
8oz Rump Steak	23
8oz Sirloin Steak	21
10oz Gammon Steak & a Free Range Egg	26
Caribbean Style Pork T-Bone Steak	16
Mixed Grill	36

Desserts

Baked Vanilla Cheesecake	18
Bramley Apple Pie	17
Bread & Butter Pudding	14
Classic Dairy Ice Cream	16
Fresh Berries	7
Fresh Fruit Salad	7
Frozen Chocolate Orange Bombe	20
Rich Chocolate Fudge Cake	19
Sharing Chocolate Trio (Half)	20
White Chocolate & Stanley Plum Tart	17

Starters

Chicken Wings	7
Gammon & Mushroom Skins	13
The Classic Prawn Cocktail	11

Side Orders

Cheesy Garlic Bread	13
Garlic Bread	10

Carvery Meats & Accompaniments, (Per Slice or Individual)

Roast Beef	5
Roast Gammon	5
Roast Pork	5
Roast Turkey	4
Stuffing Ball	4
Yorkshire Pudding	9

Vegetables, Sauces & Gravies, (Per Spoonful)

Broccoli	2
Cabbage	1
Carrots	0
Cauliflower Cheese	1
Gravy	1
Honey Glazed Parsnips	5
Leeks	1
Mashed Potato	2
Mint Sauce	2
New Potatoes	2
Parsley Sauce	1
Parsnips	4
Peas	4
Roast Potatoes	5
Swede	1

Desserts

Apple & Blackberry Pie	17
Chocolate Fudge Sensation	20
Chocolate Melting Cake	18
Dairy Ice Cream Sundae	12
Lemon Meringue Pie	16
Orange Jelly & Ice Cream	13
Toffee Apple Pie	16
Treacle Sponge	22

Starters & Sharing

Blue Cheese & Mushroom Melt	16
Bread Basket	16
Chicken Wings	17
Chorizo on Toast	12
Crayfish & Avocado Cocktail	9
Homemade Potato Wedges	14
Larder Board, to share (Half)	14
Mezze Board, to share (Half)	15
Pork & Herb Pâté	12

Salads & Pasta

Goat's Cheese Salad	17
Grilled Vegetable Pasta	20
Roast Chicken & Bacon Pasta	25
Roast Chicken Caesar Salad	16
Rocket & Crayfish Deli Salad	7

Pub Classics

BBQ Ribs	35
Chicken Jalfrezi	23
Classic Bangers & Mash	31
Ham & Eggs	17
Hand Battered Fish & Chips	30
Homemade Lasagne	17
Scampi Supper	27
Somerset Roast Chicken & Ham Pie	22
Steak & Tanglefoot Pie	28

Grill

8oz British Sirloin Steak	31
Chargilled 8oz British Rump Steak	29
Chicken & Bacon Burger	31
Gammon Steak	24
Gourmet Burger	34
Gourmet Lamb Burger	38
Grilled Pesto Marinated Vegetable Skewers	16

Our Favourites

Grilled Calves Liver	26
Our Famous Sussex Smokey	34
Roast Butternut Squash	7
Sticky Lemon Chicken	16
Grilled Tuna Steak	11

Sides

Bowl of Chips	16
Crusty Roll and Butter	7

Starters

Breaded Mushrooms	8
Crackerjack King Prawns	8
Filo Lamb Kofta	17
Flame-Grilled Chicken Wings	8
Fried Camembert	8
Harvest Feastival (for two)	27
Leek & Potato Soup	2
Nachos for One	25
Roast Vegetable & Crème Fraiche Soup	3
The Harvester Prawn Cocktail	15
Winter Vegetable & Pearl Barley Soup	2

Flamed Chicken

Barbecue Chicken & Bacon	17
Chicken & Mash	13
Chilli & Red Onion Spitroast	19
Hot Piri Piri Spitroast	19
Kickin' Garlic Spitroast	24
Mojo Spitroast	20
Simply Chicken	15
The Original Combo	26
The Original Spitroast	20

Platters

Combine Harvester, for one	37
Combine Harvester, to share (Half)	32
Personal Plantation	38
Plantation Platter, for two (Half)	33

Steaks, Grills & Classics

6oz Fillet Steak	28
8oz Rump Steak	22
8oz Sirloin Steak	23
10oz Ribeye Steak	30
12oz Rump Steak	31
Chilli & Garlic Ribs	28
Duck with Orange Sauce	21
Gammon Steak with Pineapple	21
Gammon Steak with Two Fried Eggs	22
Harvester Mixed Grill	25
Lamb Shoulder	23
Lamb Steak	13
Sausage & Mash	21
Surf & Turf	33
The Great Harvester Rack of Ribs	32

Burgers

Bacon Burger	33
BBQ Stack Burger	42
Chicken Burger	25
Harvester Burger	30
Sweet Potato Burger	33

Fish, Vegetarian & Pasta

Fish, Chips & Peas	31
Flame-Grilled Salmon	14
Flame-Grilled Tuna Steak	13
Grilled Sea Bass	15
Scampi & Chips	26
Simply Pasta	20
Totally Stuffed Mushrooms	15

Sides, Sauces & Dressings

Beer Battered Onion Rings, to share (Half)	4
Blackened Shropshire Blue Sauce	1
Blue Cheese Dressing	6
Button Mushrooms, to share (Half)	2
Cheesy Garlic Bread	11
Chilli Dough Balls	5
Crisp Seasoned Fries, to share (Half)	6
Dough Balls	6
Fresh Mashed Potato, to share (Half)	5
Garlic Bread	8
Honey & Mustard or Red Devil Dressing	2
Peppercorn Sauce	2
Reduced Fat Mayonnaise	4
Sampler of Sides, to share (Half)	8
Thousand Island Dressing	3
Wiltshire Forestiere Sauce	3

Terribly Tempting Desserts

Almond Cream Pastry	9
Apple Pie with Custard	14
Apple Pie with Ice Cream	16
Brownie & Ice Cream	20
Fresh Fruit Skewers	11
Honeycombe Explosion	21
Lemon Blizzard	21
Lime & Ginger Cheesecake	14
Pear & Ginger Pudding	18
Profiteroles	16
Rocky Horror	18
Sundae Best with Belgian Chocolate or Toffee Sauce	7
Sundae Best with Black Cherry Sauce	6
Sundae Best with Raspberry or Strawberry Sauce	9

Pickers & Sharers

Beer Battered Cod Goujons	**10**
Breaded Calamari	**10**
Chicken Wings	**6**
Chilli Beef Nachos	**11**
Grilled Prawn Skewers	**2**
Houmous Dip with Vegetables & Pitta	**8**
Irish Pork & Herb Sausage Skewers	**9**
Nachos with Cheese & Sour Cream	**15**
O'Neill's Combo (Half)	**19**
Potato Wedges with Bacon & Irish Cheddar	**13**
Potato Wedges with Mushrooms & Irish Cheddar	**10**
Quorn Sausage Skewers	**6**

Grills

BBQ Chicken Breast	**30**
Blackened Salmon	**22**
Gammon Steak	**28**
Half Rack of BBQ Ribs & Chicken Breast	**38**
Mixed Grill	**34**
Mixed Grill with a Fried Egg	**37**

Burgers

BBQ Burger	**43**
Chicken Breast & Bacon	**29**
Chilli Beef	**38**
Classic Beef	**36**
Classic Chicken Breast	**26**
Deluxe Burger	**44**
Lentil & Spinach Burger	**37**
Mixed Grill Burger	**41**

Pub Classics

All Day Irish Breakfast	**33**
All Day Vegetarian Breakfast	**24**
Bantry Bay Mussels	**17**
Breaded Scampi	**26**
Guinness Battered Fish & Chips	**30**
Seafood Crock Pot	**26**

Pies

Chicken & Limerick Ham Pie with Chips	**31**
Steak & Guinness Pie with Chips	**32**

Irish Steaks

8oz Irish Rump Steak	**23**
8oz Irish Sirloin Steak	**21**
O'Neill's Double Burger	**55**
Two Cheese Burger	**44**

Jackets

Bacon	**20**
Baked Beans	**19**
Chilli Beef	**23**
Coleslaw	**22**
Irish Cheddar	**23**
Tuna Mayonnaise	**24**

Sandwiches

BBQ Chicken, Bacon & Irish Cheddar Melt	**31**
Blackened Chicken	**22**
BLT	**25**
Irish Cheddar & Ballymaloe Relish Melt	**26**
Irish Pork & Herb Sausages with Onions	**27**
Irish Rump Steak with Onions	**28**
Quorn Sausages with Onions	**21**
Tuna & Irish Cheddar Melt	**25**

Salads

Blackened Salmon	**20**
Blackened Chicken Breast & Bacon	**22**
Mushroom & Cashel Blue Cheese	**22**

Side Dishes

Chips	**12**
Colcannon	**7**
Coleslaw	**6**
Garlic Bread	**6**
Garlic Bread with Melted Irish Cheddar	**12**
Jacket Potato with Butter	**10**
New Potatoes	**6**
Onion Rings	**8**
Side Salad (no Dressing)	**0**
Wedges	**6**

Small Plates & Sandwiches with Salad

Chilli Baguette	21
Fish Finger Buttie	22
Ham & Mature Cheddar Baguette	19
Hummous & Wood Roasted Pepper Ciabatta	21
Italian Salami & Mozzarella Baguette	21
Lemon Chicken Wrap	18
P&P Club Sandwich	22
Smoked Haddock & Spring Onion Fishcakes	10
Steak Ciabatta	20

Grazing & Sharing

Baby Bangers & Mash	12
Breaded Mushrooms	14
Bruschetta	8
Char-Grilled Mini Chorizo & Chips	13
Chicken & Chorizo Skewers	12
Chilli & Chips	16
Chips	12
Chips with Melted Cheese	20
Chips with Sour Cream	15
Chips with Sweet Chilli Dip	14
Crispy Potato Skins with Bacon & Melted Cheese	14
Falafels	14
Garlic Grilled Ciabatta	13
Homemade Fish Fingers	8
House Salad	9
Mini Whitby Scampi & Chips	15
Olives & Feta	9
Salt & Pepper Calamari	11
Spicy Chicken Wings	10
Whitebait	15

To Share

Baked Camembert (Half)	11
Mediterranean Sharer (Half)	12
Nachos (Half)	11
P&P Sharer (Half)	12

Salad & Pasta

Chicken, Bacon & Guacamole	18
Chicken Caesar	18
Marinated Lamb Rump	18
Roasted Vegetable Rigatoni	17
Smoked Salmon Linguini	20
Summer Salad	14

Our Fresh Range of Burgers

BBQ Burger	51
Blue Cheese Burger	47
Classic P&P Burger, 4oz	33
Classic P&P Burger, 8oz	40
Chicken, Bacon & Guacamole Burger	39
Chilli Burger	52
Falafel Burger	42
The New Yorker	55

P&P Favourites & Grills

10oz 28 day Matured British Rump Steak	35
10oz Char-Grilled Gammon Steak	28
Classic Steak & Ale Pie	33
Fish & Chips	34
Pan-Fried Chicken Breast	21
Pan-Fried Sea Bass	21
Sausage & Mash	23
Smoked Haddock & Spring Onion Fish Cakes	23

Desserts

Chocolate Brownie	25
Eton Mess	18
Farmhouse Apple Tartlet	21
Ice Cream	12
Lemon Cheesecake	17

Starters & Snacks

Bread & Houmous	12
Bread & Olives	8
Chicken, Chorizo & Pepper Skewers	13
Cream Cheese Stuffed Peppers	15
Crispy Fried Potato Wedges	18
Crispy Fried Potato Wedges with Bacon & Cheddar	26
Crispy Fried Potato Wedges with Beef Chilli con Carne & Cheddar	27
Garlic & Ciabatta Bread Sticks	7
Southern Fried Chicken Breast	11
Tempura Prawns	5
Tomato & Mozzarella	9
Wasabi Tempura Mixed Vegetables	4

Sharing

Crispy Duck Platter, to share (Quarter)	15
Nachos, to share (Quarter)	10
Nachos with Beef Chilli con Carne, to share (Quarter)	11
The Mezze Platter, to share (Quarter)	12
The Ultimate Platter, to share (Quarter)	14

Sandwiches & Wraps

Aromatic Duck Wrap	14
BBQ Chicken Cheddar & Bacon Sandwich	21
Croque Monsiuer	21
Grilled Chicken Wrap	11
Grilled Rump Steak Sandwich	20
Southern Fried Style Chicken Wrap	16
The BLT Sandwich	16
The FLT Wrap	15

Tostados

Chargrilled Chicken & Melted Mozzarella	25
Goat's Cheese & Roasted Vegetables	20
Spicy Chorizo & Roquito Pepper	23

Chicken Dishes

Chicken Milanese	28
Chicken Souvlaki	28
Chicken Tikka Makhani	26
Italian Style Chicken	17

Vegetarian Dishes

Butternut Squash Spinach & Goat's Cheese Lasagne	24
Channa Daal	17
Mushroom Risotto	16
Penne Arrabiata	15
Tagliatelle Primavera	18

Meat

8oz Grilled Rump Steak	**26**
8oz Grilled Rump Steak with Garlic Butter	**30**
8oz Grilled Rump Steak with Peppercorn Sauce	**29**
Beef Chilli con Carne	**27**
Cottage Pie	**25**
Gammon & Eggs	**27**
Lincolnshire Pork Sausages	**27**
Steak & Mushroom Pie with Buttery Mash	**22**
Steak & Mushroom Pie with Chips	**25**

Fish

British Wholetail Scampi	**28**
Grilled Salmon with Lemon & Black Pepper Butter	**22**
Hand Battered Fillet of Fish	**33**
Smoked Haddock Salmon & King Prawn Pie	**22**

Burgers

Bacon & Cheddar Burger	**45**
Classic Beef Burger	**37**
Falafel Burger	**32**
Grilled Chicken Fillet Burger	**25**
Mexican Burger	**31**
Reggae Reggae Chicken Burger	**27**
Ultimate Beef Burger	**48**
Ultimate Beef Burger with an Extra Beef Burger	**64**

Pasta & Risotto

Baked Linguini Carbonara	**17**
Butternut Squash Spinach & Goat's Cheese Lasagne	**24**
Chicken & Mushroom Risotto	**20**
Tagliatelle Primavera	**18**
Tagliatelle Primavera with a Grilled Chicken Fillet	**22**
Tagliatelle Primavera with a Grilled Salmon Fillet	**24**

Salads

Chargrilled Chicken Caesar	**19**
Grilled Salmon	**17**
Moroccan Chicken	**25**
Smoked Haddock Fishcakes	**17**
Summer Salad	**16**

Side Orders

Beer-Battered Onion Rings	**14**
Buttery Mash	**8**
Coleslaw	**4**
Large Chips	**22**
Seasonal Potatoes	**6**
Toasted Garlic Ciabatta Strips	**7**

Starters & Sides

Bacon & Cheese Potato Skins, no Dip	14
Broccoli & Cheddar Soup	5
Brown Multigrain or Durum Wheat Roll	9
Chicken Tikka	6
Cream of Tomato Soup	5
Garlic & Cheese Bread	13
Garlic Bread	10
Mini Poppadom	2
Roast Garlic Mushrooms	12
Sharing Baked Camembert	12
Sharing Potato Skins	13
Smoked Haddock & Spring Onion Fish Cakes	15
Thai King Prawns, no Dip	2
The Classic Prawn Cocktail	11

Meat & Trimmings

Gammon	5
Horseshoe of Pork	5
Leg of Lamb	5
Peppered Rib Eye of Beef	7
Stuffing	4
Turkey with Orange Glaze	4
Yorkshire Pudding (New Muffin Style)	9

Sauces & Gravies

Gravy, Parsley Sauce or Poultry Gravy	1
Mint Sauce	2
Vegetarian Gravy	0

Vegetables, Potatoes & Rice (Per Spoonful)

Baby Jacket Potatoes	1
Basmati Rice	3
Bombay, Mashed or New Potatoes	2
Broccoli (with Butter)	2
Cabbage	1
Caramelised Onion Gravy	2
Carrots & Spinach, Swede or Leeks	1
Cauliflower Cheese	1
Dauphinoise Potatoes	3
Honey Glazed Parsnips	5
Noodles	1
Parsnips	4
Peas	4
Peas & Asparagus	1
Pilau Rice	4
Rice & Peas	1
Roast Potatoes	5

Pubs & Carveries **Toby Carvery**

Carvery Alternatives & Pub Food

Beef Jalfrezi	19
Boston Bean Hash, without Vegetables	3
Carvery Beef Pie	14
Carvery Turkey & Gammon Pie	12
Chicken Tikka Salad	17
Chilli con Carne	13
Cod Fillet in Cheese Sauce, without Vegetables	6
Farmer's Platter	22
Lemon & Pepper Chicken Salad	6
Mushroom Lasagne	22
Parmesan Crusted Cod, without Vegetables	4
Ploughman's	40
Roast Potatoes with Cheese	17
Roast Potatoes with Chilli	12
Roast Potatoes with Chilli & Cheese	14
Sausage & Mash	29
Sea Bass, without Vegetables	7
Seafood Salad	21
Spicy Vegetable Crumble	8
Turkey Jalfrezi	15
Yellow Fin Sole, without Vegetables	4

Specials

BBQ Chicken Pieces	11
Beef Piri Piri	13
Beef Stroganoff	17
Cajun Chicken	8
Chicken Makhani	11
Chilli con Carne	11
Lemon Chicken Pieces	10
Morrocan Lamb	8
Mushroom & Spinach Curry	4
Sweet & Sour Pork	10

Desserts

Bramley Apple Crumble, without Custard	18
Chocolate Brownie Ice Cream Sensation	20
Chocolate Fudge Cake	18
Dairy Ice Cream Sundae	12
Honeycomb Dream Sundae	20
Jam Suet Sponge, without Custard	15
Madagascan Cheescake	15
Raspberry & White Chocolate Pavlova	12
Treacle Sponge	22
Triple Strawberry Sundae	29
Waffles with Cherries	24

Breakfast

Baked Beans on Toast	14
Blueberry Muffin	13
Chocolate Muffin	14
Large Breakfast with Toast	46
Morning Roll with Bacon	15
Morning Roll with Fried Egg	16
Morning Roll with Sausage	14
Morning Roll with Vegetarian Sausage	11
Scrambled Egg on Toast	14
Toast & Preserves	12
Traditional Breakfast	25
Vegetarian Breakfast	22

Starters & Sharers

Breaded Mushrooms	14
Buffalo Chicken Wings	41
Caesar Salad	7
Nachos (Half)	18
Nachos with Chilli con Carne (Half)	21
Nachos with Five Bean Chilli (Half)	20
Reggae Reggae Chicken Nachos (Half)	22
Spicy Coated King Prawns	7
Tomato & Basil Soup with Malted Grain Baguette & Butter	16
Tomato & Basil Soup with White Poppy Seed Bloomer	11
Tomato & Basil Soup without Bread	5
Wetherspoon Sharer (Half)	36

JDW Deli

BBQ Chicken & Bacon Melt Ciabatta or Panini	17
BBQ Chicken & Bacon Melt Malted Grain Baguette	18
BLT Ciabatta	20
BLT Malted Grain Baguette	21
Chicken Wrap with Chicken Breast Slices	10
Mature Cheddar Cheese & Pickle Ciabatta	18
Mature Cheddar Cheese & Pickle Malted Grain Baguette	19
Mature Cheddar Cheese & Tomato Panini	19
Portion of Chips	10
Southern Fried Chicken Wrap	14
Steak Ciabatta with Chips	31
Tuna Mayonnaise Ciabatta	15
Tuna Mayonnaise Malted Grain Baguette	16
Wiltshire Ham & Mature Cheddar Cheese Panini	22
Wiltshire Ham Ciabatta	13
Wiltshire Ham Malted Grain Baguette	14

Value Meals

Bacon Carbonara	27
Breaded Plaice with Chips & Peas	22

Chicken, Leek & Wiltshire Ham Pie with Chips, Peas & Gravy	35
Chilli con Carne with Yellow Basmati Rice & Tortilla Chips	23
Cottage Pie with Chips & Peas	23
Fish, Chips & Peas with Tartare Sauce (Cod)	27
Five Bean Chilli – with Yellow Basmati Rice & Tortilla Chips	16
Ham, Eggs & Chips	18
Lasagne al Forno with Dressed Salad	22
Meatballs with Linguine Pasta	17
Sausage, Chips & Beans	25
Spicy Tomato Pasta	12
Vegetarian Sausages, Chips & Beans	20
Wetherspoon Ploughman's	31

Jacket Potatoes

Baked Beans	19
Chilli con Carne, Sour Cream & a Dressed Side Salad	21
Five Bean Chilli	18
Mature Cheddar Cheese & a Dressed Side Salad	22
Tuna Mayonnaise	24

Main Meals

8oz Gammon Steak with Eggs, Chips & Pineapple	28
8oz Sirloin Steak with Chips, Peas, Tomato & a Flat Mushroom	32
8oz Sirloin Steak with a Jacket Potato & Butter & a Dressed Salad	33
10oz Rump Steak with Chips, Peas, Tomato & a Flat Mushroom	29
10oz Rump Steak with a Jacket Potato & Butter & a Dressed Side Salad.	31
BBQ Chicken Melt with Chips, Peas, Tomato & a Flat Mushroom	28
BBQ Chicken Melt with a Jacket Potato & a Dressed Side Salad	29
Braised Shoulder of Lamb with Mashed Potato & Vegetables	36
British Beef & Abbot Ale Pie served with Chips, Vegetables & Gravy	37
British Beef & Abbot Ale Pie served with Mashed Potato, Vegetables & Gravy	40
Butternut Squash & Fire-Roasted Tomato Risotto with Garlic Bread	19
Butternut Squash & Fire-Roasted Tomato Risotto with a Side Salad	15
Chicken Caesar Salad	18
Chicken Pasta Alfredo with a Dressed Side Salad	19
Chicken Pasta Alfredo with Garlic Bread	18
Chicken Tikka Masala	27
Creamy Peppercorn Steak Sauce	3
Half Roast Chicken	32
Large Mixed Grill with Chips, Peas, Tomato & a Flat Mushroom	51
Large Mixed Grill with a Jacket Potato & a Dressed Side Salad	53
Mixed Grill with Chips, Peas, Tomatoes & a Flat Mushroom	37
Salmon Fillet with Hollandaise Sauce served with Chips & Vegetables	26
Salmon Fillet with Hollandaise Sauce with a Jacket Potato & a Dressed Side Salad	31

Sausages & Mash with Red Wine & Onion Gravy	27
Surf n Turf – Rump Steak, Spicy Coated King Prawns, Chips, Peas, Tomato & Sweet Chilli Dip	34
Vegetarian Sausages & Mash	22
Warm Chicken & Bacon Salad	16
Wholetail Breaded Scampi	27

Burgers

6oz Classic Beef Burger with Chips	31
Breaded Chicken Burger with Chips	24
Gourmet Beef Burger with Chips	48
Gourmet Chicken Burger with Chips	40
Gourmet Vegetable Burger with Chips	33
Vegetable Burger with Chips	23

Sides

Beer Battered Onion Rings (Large)	16
Bowl of Chips	21
Bowl of Chips topped with Cheddar Cheese	28
Bowl of Chips topped with Chilli con Carne	26
Bowl of Chips topped with Five Bean Chilli	24
Garlic Ciabatta Bread	6
Garlic Ciabatta Bread with Cheese	13
Mixed Vegetables	2
Side Salad with Dressing (no Croutons)	4
Side Salad with Dressing & Croutons	6

Steak Club

10oz Rump Steak with Chips, Peas, Tomatoes & a Flat Mushroom	29
10oz Rump Steak with a Jacket Potato & a Dressed Side Salad	31
8oz Sirloin Steak with a Jacket Potato, Butter & a Dressed Salad	33
BBQ Chicken Melt with Chips, Peas, Tomato & a Flat Mushroom	28
BBQ Chicken Melt with a Jacket Potato & a Dressed Side Salad	29
Beer Battered Whole Onion Rings	16
Gammon Steak & Pineapple served with a Jacket Potato & a Dressed Side Salad	27
Gammon Steak & Pineapple with Chips, Peas, Tomato & a Flat Mushroom	21
Gammon Steak with Egg served with Chips, Peas, Tomato & a Flat Mushroom	22
Gammon Steak with Egg served with a Jacket Potato & a Dressed Side Salad	29
Mixed Grill with Chips, Peas, Tomato & a Flat Mushroom	37
Mixed Grill with a Jacket Potato & a Dressed Side Salad	39
Salmon Fillet with Hollandaise Sauce with Chips, Peas, Tomato & a Flat Mushroom	26
Scampi	13
Stilton, Shropshire Blue & Spring Onion Sauce	3

Curry Club

Beef Madras (Complete Meal)	35
Bombay Potatoes (Complete Meal)	6
Chicken Biryani Meal with Naan Bread	24
Chicken Jalfrezi Meal with Naan Bread	25
Chicken Korma Meal with Naan Bread	30
Chicken Tikka Masala Meal with Naan Bread	28
Chicken Vindaloo (Complete Meal)	27
Hot Chicken Masala Meal with Naan Bread	28
King Prawn Thai Curry	23
Lamb Kashmiri with Naan Bread	33
Lamb Rogan Josh Meal with Naan Bread	28
Lamb Samosa	5
Luxury Chicken Tikka Masala	27
Onion Bhaji	4
Poppadums & Dips	10
Sweet Potato, Chickpea & Spinach Curry with Extra Poppadums	25
Sweet Potato, Chickpea & Spinach Curry with Naan Bread	30
Vegetable Samosa	3

Sunday Club

Cauliflower Cheese	6
Creamy Mashed Potato	10
Half Roast Chicken	37
Portobello Mushroom, Chickpea & Pumpkin Seed Roast	29
Roast Pork served with Roast Potatoes, Yorkshire Pudding & Vegetables	28
Roast Potatoes	8
Sage & Onion Stuffing Balls (2)	3
Vegetables	2
Yorkshire Puddings (2)	4

Desserts

Belgian Waffle with Fruit Compote	15
Bramley Apple, Pear & Raspberry Crumble with Vanilla Ice Cream	18
Chocolate Brownie Sundae	25
Chocolate Fudge Cake with Vanilla Ice Cream	21
Mint Chocolate Ice Cream Bombe	8
Sticky Toffee Pudding with Custard	19

Sandwiches

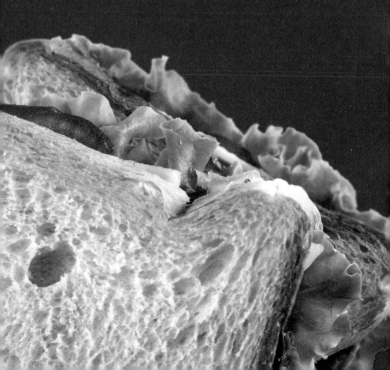

Asda

All Day Breakfast	13
BLT	9
Cheese & Onion	12
Cheese & Spring Onion	16
Cheese & Tomato, No Mayo	9
Cheese Ploughman's	10
Chicken & Stuffing	13
Chicken & Sweetcorn	10
Chicken Fajita Wrap, No Mayo	10
Chicken Salad	10
Chicken Tikka & Onion Bhaji Wrap	12
Chicken, Bacon & Caesar Wrap	12
Egg & Cress Reduced Fat	8
Egg Mayonnaise	9
Egg Salad	9
Egg Salad, Deep Fill	10
Good For You – Prawn Mayonnaise	6
Good For You – Smoked Ham & Mustard	7
Ham Cheese & Pickle, No Mayo	12
Ham, No Mayo	7
Nacho Chicken Wrap, No Mayo	10
New York Deli	8
Peking Duck Wrap, No Mayo	11
Poached Salmon & Horseradish	9
Prawn Mayo Triple	12
Red Leicestershire Salad	10
Salmon & Cucumber	8
Southern Fried Chicken Wrap	12
Topside of Beef & Caramelised Onions	8
Tuna & Cucumber Reduced Fat	7

Kraft

Philadelphia Light with Dry Cured Ham	9
Philadelphia Light with Roasted Peppers	10

M&S

Bacon, Lettuce & Tomato	16
Beef & Rocket Baguette	13
Brie & Rocket Baguette	16
Cheddar Cheese & Celery	15
Cheddar Cheese Ploughman's	14
Cheese & Onion	6
Cheese & Tomato Roll	6
Egg & Bacon Baguette	16
Fuller for Longer British Chicken & Bacon on Malted Bread	11
Ham & Cheese Baguette	14
Hoisin Duck Wrap	12
Italian Mozzarella, Tomatoes, Pesto & Spinach Roll	15

Mexican 3 Bean Wrap	12
Mexican Chicken Wrap	15
Mini Chicken Salad Baguette	7
Mini Egg & Tomato Baguette	8
Mini Smoked Salmon & Cream Cheese Baguette	8
Organic Egg & Watercress	12
Organic Herby Roast Chicken	14
Organic Poached Salmon & Spinach	16
Prawn & Mayonnaise	11
Simply Salad	9

M&S – Count on Us

Bacon Lettuce & Tomato	7
British Ham Salad & Mustard Dressing on Oatmeal Bread	7
Chicken & Mustard Camapaillou	7
Chicken Tikka	7
Chilli Beef Wrap	7
Jalfrezi Chicken Chapatti	6
Lean Danish Ham Salad	6
Prawn Mayonnaise	6
Rancher's Chicken Flatbread	7
Roast Chicken Sandwich, No Mayo	7
Smoked Ham Cheese & Pickle	7

M&S – Eat Well

British Roast Chicken & Sweetcorn	9
Chicken & Salad	11
Free Range Egg & Watercress	9
Poached Salmon	9
Prawn Mayonnaise	8
Rare Roast British Beef & Horseradish Mayonnaise	11
Tuna & Sweetcorn	10

M&S – Food To Go

Cheese & Coleslaw	16
The Big Bacon, Lettuce & Tomato, Prawn & Mayo, Ham, Cheese & Pickle	19
The Big Chicken & Sweetcorn, Chicken Salad, Chicken & Stuffing	17
The Big Egg & Cress, Prawn & Mayo, Smoked Ham & Mustard, Salmon & Cucumber	19
The Big Prawn & Mayo, Tuna & Sweetcorn, Seafood Cocktail	19
Wensleydale & Carrot	12
Tuna Baguette	14

Sainsbury's

All Day Breakfast	13
BBQ Steak Wrap	11
Beef Roll	13
Big Bacon & Tomato, Chicken Salad, Double Gloucester & Onion	17

	ProPoints value
Big Chargrilled Chicken Caesar Sub Roll	17
Big Chicken Tikka, Thai & Korma	15
Big Mature Cheddar & Tomato	15
Big Pork Sausage & Egg	20
Big Prawn Mayonnaise	17
Big Roast Chicken Salad	16
Brunch Triple	16
Cheddar Cheese, Philadelphia & Celery	13
Cheese & Tomato	10
Cheese Ploughman's Baguette	15
Chicken & Bacon Salad	11
Chicken & Chorizo	10
Chicken & Stuffing	10
Chicken Fajita Wrap	12
Deep Fill BLT	12
Egg & Cress	9
Egg Mayonnaise & Cress	10
Free Range Egg & Watercress	11
Ham Salad	9
Ham, Cheese & Pickle Wrap	13
Lunch Triple	12
Meatball Baguette	15
Mini Roll Selection – Egg Mayonaise & Cress	4
Mini Roll Selection – Ham & Soft Cheese	4
Mini Roll Selection – Roast Chicken with Mayonnaise	3
Prawn Mayonnaise	9
Roast Chicken Salad Baguette	12
Roast Chicken Salad Wrap	12
Smoked Ham & Mustard	6
Southern Fried Chicken Wrap	12
Steak & Onion Baguette	12
Taste The Difference Salt Beef with Pickled Gherkins & Mustard Mayo	14
Tuna & Sweetcorn	13

Sainsbury's – Be Good To Yourself

Cheese Ploughman's	9
Deep Filled Beef & Horseradish	9
Deep Filled Chargrilled Chicken Salsa	6
Egg & Cress	7
Honey & Mustard Chicken Salad in a Soft Wrap	9
Mexican Style Bean in a Soft Multigrain Wrap	11
Roast Chicken Salad	7
Salmon & Cucumber	7
Triple BLT, Chicken & Double Gloucester	12
Tuna & Cucumber	8

Tesco

Bacon, Lettuce & Tomato, Malted Brown Bread	14
Big & Tasty Ham, Cheese & Mustard	15

	ProPoints value
Big & Tasty Spicy Chicken	11
Cajun Chicken Wrap	12
Cheese & Bacon Club	12
Cheese & Onion Brown Bread	14
Cheese & Pickle	10
Cheese Triple	19
Chicken & Bacon Sub	13
Chicken & Bacon Wrap	15
Chicken & Sweetcorn	10
Chicken, Bacon & Lettuce, Brown Bread	13
Chicken Caesar	11
Chicken Caesar Wrap	13
Chicken Fajita Wrap	11
Chicken Salad	10
Chicken Triple	15
Egg & Cress	11
Egg & Cress Triple	16
Egg & Tomato Sandwich	8
Egg & Bacon, Malted Brown Bread	13
Free Range Egg Florentine	11
Ham & Cheddar Sub	14
Ham & Mustard Roll	7
Ham Cheese & Pickle, Brown Bread	12
Hoisin Duck Wrap	9
Indian Chicken Balti Wrap	10
Indian Chicken Korma Wrap	14
Indian Chicken Tikka Masala Wrap	5
Indian Onion Bhaji Wrap	16
Pesto Chicken	11
Prawn Mayonnaise	8
Prawn Mayonnaise, Oatmeal Bread	10
Prawn Mayonnaise Triple	14
Red Cheddar & Tomato	13
Roast Chicken & Stuffing	13
Roast Chicken	10
Salmon & Cucumber	8
Salmon & Rocket	12
Sausage & Egg Sandwich	14
Sausage Bacon & Egg Triple	19
Seafood Cocktail	10
Smoked Ham & Cheddar	12
Smoked Ham & Mustard	7
Southern Fried Chicken	10
Southern Fried Chicken Wrap	12
Tuna & Cucumber	10
Tuna Sweetcorn, Malt Bread	9

Tesco – Light Choices

Chicken & Bacon	9
Chicken & Stuffing	8

Chicken Salad	7
Chicken Salsa on Tomato Bread	7
Chicken, Bacon & Lettuce	9
Chicken, Tomato & Herb	8
Egg & Cress	7
Egg Salad	7
Ham & Cheese	8
Ham Salad	7
Ploughman's	9
Prawn Mayonnaise	7
Roast Chicken & Stuffing	7
Salmon & Cucumber	7
Thai Chicken	8

The Co-Operative

Aberdeen Angus Beef with Vine Ripened Tomato & Rocket	10
Aromatic Duck Wrap	10
BBQ Pork Wrap	12
BLT, Prawn Mayonnaise, Chicken Salad Triple Pack	13
Breakfast Sub Roll	15
Brie, Sweetcure Bacon & Apple & Grape Chutney	12
British Pork, Red Cabbage & Chutney	12
Broad Bean & Spinach Falafel Wrap	12
Cheese	11
Cheese & Onion	12
Cheese & Tomato	12
Chicken & Bacon Caesar Wrap	14
Chicken & Bacon Sub Roll	11
Chicken & Herb Salad	11
Chicken & Sweetcorn	7
Chicken Fajita Wrap	11
Chicken Salad	8
Chicken Sandwich Triple Pack	14
Chicken Tikka & Onion Bhaji	12
Classic BLT	9
Coriander & Coconut Chicken	11
Cumberland Sausage & Spicy Chutney	13
Deep Fill All Day Breakfast	12
Deep Fill BLT	12
Deep Fill Cheese Ploughman's	13
Deep Fill Chicken, Bacon & Tomato	13
Deep Fill Chicken Salad	8
Deep Fill Chicken, Stuffing & Red Onion	11
Deep Fill Egg & Bacon	15
Deep Fill Ham, Cheese & Pickle	11
Deep Fill Italian Mozzarella Cheese & Tomato	13
Deep Fill Tuna & Sweetcorn	11
Feta Cheese & Salad	12
Food to Go – Cheese & Onion	12
Food to Go – Chicken Tikka Baguette	16

Food to Go – Free Range Egg Mayonnaise Baguette	12
Food to Go – Prawn Mayonnaise Baguette	15
Food to Go – Red Pesto Chicken Baguette	15
Food to Go – Southern Fried Chicken Baguette	16
Food to Go – Tuna Mayonnaise Baguette	14
Food to Go – Turkey, Stuffing & Cranberry Baguette	12
Free Range Egg & Cress	10
Free Range Egg Mayonnaise	11
Ham & Cheese	11
Ham Salad	8
Ham	7
Houmous & Crudite Wrap	11
Goat's Cheese & Caramelised Shallot	12
King Prawn & Ginger Mayonnaise	9
Mackerel Salad	12
Meatball Sub	11
Mediterranean Tuna	10
Mixed Triple Sandwich (BLT, Prawn Mayo, Chicken Salad)	14
Mozzarella & Tomato Sandwich Deep Fill	12
New York Deli	11
Piri Piri Chicken Wrap	11
Prawn Mayonnaise	8
Prawn Mayonnaise, Turkey & Stuffing, Cheddar Cheese & Chutney Triple Pack	16
Red Pesto Chicken	11
Salmon & Cucumber	8
Southern Fried Chicken Wrap	11
Tuna & Sweetcorn	8
Tuna Mayonnaise	8
Wensleydale, Beetroot & Horseradish Relish	11

The Co-Operative – Healthy Living

Chicken & Bacon	6
Chicken Salad	7
Chicken Tikka	7
Chicken Tikka Wrap	7
Prawn Mayonnaise	7
Soft Cheese & Roasted Red Pepper	8
Tuna & Cucumber	7

The Co-Operative – Truly Irresistible

Aberdeen Angus Beef with Horseradish & Mustard Baguette	15
Aberdeen Angus Beef with Vine Ripened Tomato & Rocket	9
Aberdeen Angus Beef, Taw Valley Mature Cheddar & Caramelised Onion Focaccia	12
Chicken & Sweetcure Bacon	15
Denhay Mature Cheddar Cheese & Plum Chutney	13
Smoked Salmon, Cucumber & Watercress	10
Taw Valley Cheese Baguette	17
Wiltshire Ham Baguette	13

Waitrose

Atlantic Prawns with Creamy Mayonnaise	11
Beef with Horseradish Mayonnaise & Rocket on Malted Bread	11
Breakfast Panini	14
British Ham with English Mustard	9
Cheese Ploughman's	12
Chicken Caesar Salad Wrap with Smoky Sweetcure Bacon & Parmigiano Reggiano	14
Chicken Fajita Wrap	8
Chicken, no Mayonnaise	9
Crayfish & Rocket	9
Croque Monsieur	12
Egg Mayo & Baby Watercress on Malted Bread with Seeds	14
Egg Mayo & Bacon	15
Egg Mayo with Cress	11
Egg Mayo with Crunchy Salad	8
Grilled Vegetable & Houmous Wrap with Baby Spinach, Crunchy Carrot & Pine Nuts	12
Irish Mature Cheddar with Crunchy Red Onion & Mayonaise	10
Irish Mature Cheddar with Vine Ripened Tomatoes	11
Lamb Tabbouleh Flatbread	9
Mature Cheddar Ploughman's with Davidstow Cheddar, Pickled Onions & Chutney	14
Mozzarella & Roast Tomato Wrap	16
Mozzarella & Tomato	10
Mozzarella, Chicken, Bacon & Mushroom Panini	14
Prawn Mayonnaise	13
Roast Chicken & Bacon with Dijon Mustard Mayonnaise	10
Roast Chicken with Leaves, Tomatoes, Cucumber & Mayonnaise	12
Roast Chicken with Sage & Onion Stuffing on Malted Bread	9
Sandwich Selection	10
Seafood Salad	5
Smoked Salmon & Soft Cheese	13
Tuna & Mayo with Cucumber	13
Tuna & Celery	7
Tuna Mayo & Crunchy Sweetcorn	13
Wild Alaskan Salmon with Chunky Cucumber	7
Wiltshire Ham, Cheddar & Pickle	12

Waitrose – Perfectly Balanced

Chargrilled Chicken Wrap	7
Chargrilled Vegetable Wrap	9
Lemon Chicken with SunBlush Tomato Relish	6
Wiltshire Ham & Tomato	7

Spanish & Tex Mex

Starters & Tapas

Aubergine Omelette – Tortilla de Berenjenas	11
Casserole of Vermicelli – Fideos a la Cazuela	15
Clams in Matelote Sauce – Almejas a la Marinera	4
Cod Fritters – Buñuelos de Bacalao	12
Garlic Prawns – Gambas al Ajillo	9
Marinated Anchovies – Boquerónes	7
Mixed Marinated Olives – Aceitunas Mixtas	3
Mushrooms with Garlic – Champiñones al Ajillo	6
Mussels in Matelote Sauce – Mejillones a la Marinera	4
Sautéed Broad Beans with Cured Ham – Habas Salteadas con Jamón	7
Slices of Cured Serrano Ham – Jamón Serrano	3
Spanish Potato Omelette – Tortilla de Patatas a la Española	9
Spinach Cannelloni – Canelones de Espinacas	11
Spinach Omelette – Tortilla de Espinacas	6

Main Course

Black Rice – Arroz Negro	13
Chargrilled Cod – Brandada de Bacalao	13
Chicken with Garlic – Pollo al Ajillo	9
Cod in Aspic – Bacalao al Pilpil	23
Meatballs with Sauce – Albóndigas con Salsa	14
Paella with Vegetables – Paella de Verduras	13
Stuffed Peppers (with Rice & Vegetables) – Pimientos Rellenos	6

Sauces & Accompaniments

Garlic Mayonnaise – Aioli, 1 tablespoon	3
Green Salad – Ensalade Verde (no Dressing)	0
Mixed Salad – Ensalada Mixte (no Dressing)	0
Nut Bread – Pan de Nueces	5
Tomato Salad – Ensalada de Tomate (no Dressing)	0

Dessert

Catalan Crème Brûlée – Crema Catalana	14
Chocolate Mousse – Mousse de Chocolate	8
Chocolate Sponge Cake – Bizcocho de Chocolate	11
Coconut Flan – Flan de Coco	7
Cream-Filled Jelly Roll – Brazo de Gitano Relleno de Crema	6
Fruit Tart – Tarta de Frutas	9
Lemon Mousse – Mousse de Limón	5
Lemon Sherbet – Sorbete de Limón	6
Milk Meringue – Leche Merengada	6
Vanilla Sponge – Plum-cake	7

Starters & Appetisers

Bean Quesadillas (1)	5
Black Bean Soup	4
Cheese Quesadillas (1)	9
Chicken Quesadillas (1)	7
Gazpacho	6
Jalapeño Poppers (1)	8
Nachos with Cheese	17
Nachos with Cheese & Beans	18
Tortilla Soup	8

Main Courses

BBQ Ribs	22
Bean Burritos (1)	11
Beef & Bean Enchiladas	11
Beef & Potato Burritos	18
Beef Chimichangas (1)	18
Beef Empanadas (2)	15
Beef Fajita (1)	15
Beef Taco Salad	17
Beef Tacos (1)	19
Chicken Chimichangas (1)	17
Chicken Enchiladas	11
Chicken Fajita (1)	14
Classic Chilli with Beans	16
Huevos Rancheros	17
Seafood Enchiladas	10
Spinach Enchiladas	10
Veggie Wrap	7

Sides

Corn Bread	11
Frijoles Refritas	8
Grilled Corn on the Cob (1)	5
Guacamole	2
Sour Cream	2
Spanish Rice	8

Starters

Barbecue Ribs (for one)	11
Calamari or Gulf Shrimp Cocktail	11
Chicken & Corn Chowder	8
Chicken Nachos, to share (Half)	14
Chicken, Bacon & Avocado Salad	16
Chicken Wings (for one) or Chilli Poppers	11
Chipotle Meatballs	12
Deep Filled Potato Skins	11
Fiesta Nachos, to share (Half)	12
Garlic Flatbread 'Tostadas'	6
Sloppy José Nachos, to share (Half)	17

Burgers (no additional toppings)

'Bandido' Chilli Bean Burger	33
Big Texan Cowboy Burger	49
Cheese & Bacon Burger	43
Chipotle Meatball Burger	33
Chiquito's Classico Burger	42
Grilled Chicken Burger	27

Quesadillas

Cheese & Bacon Quesadilla	26
Chicken & Chorizo Quesadilla	25
Veggie Bean Quesadilla	28

North of the Border

8oz Rump Steak	25
10oz Sirloin Steak	24
'Cowboy' Beans & Bacon	28
Barbecue Rack of Ribs	25
Beer Battered Cod & Chips	38
Chicken 'n' Ribs	29
Smokin'-Texan-Chilli-Hot-Dog	36
Southern Fried Chicken	23
Texan-Chicken-Melt	25

Wraps & Salads

Acapulco Chicken Salad	15
Border Wrap	31
Cajun Beef Wrap	32
Chicken, Bacon & Avocado Salad	19
Fajita Duck Wrap	30
Fajita Roasted Vegetable Salad	10
Fiesta Vegetable Wrap	34
Jalapeño Scampi Wrap	27
Santa Fe Wrap	35
Southwest Caesar Salad	11

Pasta

Chicken in Ancho-Chilli-Tomato Sauce	20
Chipotle Meatball	25
Fajita Roasted Vegetables	15
Mac 'n' Jack	19
Spicy Tomato Chipotle	12

Fajitas

Acapulco Chicken	24
Barbecue Chicken	25
Classic Chicken	24
Duck	32
Roasted Vegetables	20
Steak	30
Tiger Prawns	22
Ultimate Fajita Feast	31

Mexican Kitchen

Beef Chilli Burritos	33
Beef Chilli Chimichangas	35
Beef Chilli Enchiladas	36
Beef Chilli Tacos	32
Cajun 'Slow Cooked' Beef Burritos	33
Cajun 'Slow Cooked' Beef Chimichangas	35
Cajun 'Slow Cooked' Beef Enchiladas	37
Cajun 'Slow Cooked' Beef Tacos	33
Fajita Roasted Vegetables Burritos	30
Fajita Roasted Vegetables Chimichangas	32
Fajita Roasted Vegetables Enchiladas	32
Fajita Roasted Vegetables Tacos	28
Shredded Duck Burritos	36
Shredded Duck Chimichangas	38
Shredded Duck Enchiladas	39
Shredded Duck Tacos	34
Spicy Chicken in Ancho-Chilli-Tomato Sauce Burritos	32
Spicy Chicken in Ancho-Chilli-Tomato Sauce Chimichangas	34
Spicy Chicken in Ancho-Chilli-Tomato Sauce Enchiladas	35
Spicy Chicken in Ancho-Chilli-Tomato Sauce Tacos	31
Vegetable Chilli Burritos	30
Vegetable Chilli Chimichangas	32
Vegetable Chilli Enchiladas	35
Vegetable Chilli Tacos	31

Sides

Beef & Bean Chilli	5
Mexican Spiced Rice	4
Onion Rings	13
Refried Beans or 'Cowboy' Baked Beans	3
Rustic Red Skin Mash or Skin-on-Fries or Baked Wedges	12

Starters

Aceitunas Mixtas	4
Cecina	9
Jamón Serrano	3
Melón Galia Y Jamón Serrano	6
Pan de Ajo	6
Pan de Ajo con Queso	10
Pan de Barra Catalán	9
Pane Arabe con Cobertura	14
Plato de Charcuteria	13

Paellas

Paella de Carne	15
Paella de Mariscos	13
Paella Valenciana	23
Paella de Verduras	23

Tapas to Share (Regular Size)

Seafood

Bacalo Confitado	7
Calamares Andaluza	18
Gambas Gabardina	16
Gambas Pil Pil	9
Langostinos a la Plancha	2
Pescado Blanco Frito	17
Salmón Fresco	9

Meat

Albóndigas a la Jardinera	16
Buey al Jerez	20
Chorizo Frito al Vino	15
Cordero de Mallorca	19
Costillas de Cerdo	14
Estofado Vasco	11

Chicken

Alitas de Pollo	7
Brochetas de Pollo	7
Croquetas de Pollo	10
Pollo con Salsa	10

Vegetables

Berenjenas Gratinadas	8
Champiñones al Ajillo	8
Champiñones Rellenos	7
Croquetas de Champiñones	7
Ensalada Verde Mixta	2
Patatas Bravas	8
Patatas Bravas con Queso	14
Pimiento Romano	9
Pisto Manchego	4
Tortilla Española	6
Verdura Fritas	9

Supermarket Cafés

Main Dishes

Asda Café Salad (no Dressing)	0
Asda Fruit Salad	1
Beef Olives	5
Bridies Pie	10
British Steak Bake	11
Celtic Pride Steak & Ale Pie	16
Cheese & Onion Quiche	16
Chicken & Mushroom Pie	14
Chicken Bhuna	10
Chicken Korma	12
Chicken Tikka	10
Chilli con Carne	9
Cornish Pasty	12
Lamb Shoulder	18
Large Sausage Roll	11
Lasagne	16
Lorne Sausage	4
Macaroni Cheese	13
Macaroni Pie	10
Mixed Vegetables	8
Onion Bhaji	2
Pilau Rice	14
Potato Cheese & Onion Pie	16
Scotch Pie	9
Steak Mushroom & Ale Pie	16
Steak Pie	16
Vegetarian Sausage Casserole	17
Welsh Beef Curry	10

Side Dishes & Accompaniments

Carrot & Peas	2
Garlic Bread Slices	3
Mashed Potato or Roast Potatoes	4
Yorkshire Pudding	10

Cakes & Desserts (Per Slice)

Baked Fruit Scone	8
Big Bramley Apple Pie	12
Caramel Shortcake	9
Carrot Cake	18
Chocolate Brownie	7
Chocolate Fudge Cake	11
Iced Ginger Squares	11
Fruit Squares	12
Lemon Meringue Pie	11
Pineapple Tarts	11
Special Vanilla Cheesecake	8
Strawberry Waffle Cheesecake	15
Victoria Sponge	12

Hot Food

Bacon Roll	12
Brie, Leek & Mushroom Melt with Side Salad & Dressing	13
Butternut Squash Soup with 2 Mini Rolls	8
Cheese & Ham Toastie	13
Cheese & Tomato Pizza	6
Chicken, Cheddar & Bacon Toastie	13
Country Vegetable Soup with 2 Mini Rolls	7
Egg & Bacon Muffin	10
Emmental Cheese & Mushroom Toastie	13
Ham Hock & Cheese Melt with Side Salad & Dressing	11
Irish Pancakes	2
Jacket Potato, No Filling	9
Jacket Potato with Baked Beans	14
Jacket Potato with Chilli Filling	16
Jacket Potato with Grated Cheese	19
Jacket Potato with Tuna & Sweetcorn	14
Lasagne with Side Salad & Dressing	18
Macaroni Cheese with Side Salad & Dressing	19
Pasta with Cherry Tomatoes, Spinach, Pine Nuts & Pecorino Cheese	12
Pea & Ham Soup with 2 Mini Rolls	12
Spaghetti Bolognese	7
Tomato & Basil Soup with 2 Mini Rolls	8

Cold Food

BLT Sandwich	11
Eat Well Egg & Watercress Sandwich	9
Eat Well New Potato Salad with Hot Smoked Salmon	7
Eat Well Red Salmon & Cucumber Sandwich	8
Eat Well Roast Chicken & Salad Sandwich	8
Ham & Cheese Croissant	10
Meat Mini Rolls	11
Prawn Cocktail	9
Roast Turkey, Cranberry & Bacon Sandwich	12
Sandwich Collection	9
Side Salad with Dressing	1

Snacks, Cakes & Sweet Treats

Apple Turnover	9
Bakewell Tart	12
Cheese Scone	9
Choc Chunk Muffin (Gluten Free)	14
Chocolate Brownie	7
Chocolate Stirrer	2
Clotted Cream	7
Cranberry & White Chocolate Flapjack	8
Croissant	6
Crumpet	3

	ProPoints value
Devon Scone	9
Eat Well Fruit Salad	2
Eccles Cake	10
Free Oat Biscuit	1
Fruit Scone	9
Fruit Slice (Gluten Free)	7
Gingerbread Boy/Girl Cookie	5
Iced Bun	7
Large Gold Coin	4
Lemon & Sultana Slice	10
Lemon Trickle Cake	14
Lightly Salted Handcooked Crisps	5
Milk Chocolate Chip Cookie	9
Millionaire Shortbread	9
Mince Pie	11
Mince Pie with Brandy Cream	12
Operetta Layer Cake	24
Pain au Raisin	12
Pecan Twist	12
Rocky Road	9
Sea Salt & Balsamic Vinegar Handcooked Crisps	5
Shortbread	3
Sticky Toffee Slice	11
Strawberry Jam	2
Sultana & Apple Flapjack	10
Teacakes	9
Victoria Layer Cake	18
White Chocolate Chip Cookie	9

Cold Drinks

Apple Juice	3
Berry Fruits Crush	2
Freshly Squeezed Lemonade	3
Glass of Whole Milk	5
Mango & Pineapple Fruit Crush	2
Orange & Raspberry Juice	3
Orange Juice	3
Pressed Apple Juice	3
Still Lemon & Lime Water	0

Cakes & Pastries

Etolie	11
Fruit Scone	12
Lemon Cheesecake	9
Miroir Cassis	7
Tarte Citron	11
Triple Chocolate Muffin	15
Tropique Mousse	7

Cold Sandwiches

Cheese & Tomato	12
Christmas Turkey with Bacon, Stuffing & Cranberry Sauce	13
Ham & Cheese Croissant	9
Marmalade Ham	4

Hot Dishes

Asparagus & Babycorn Masala	9
Beef Moussaka	18
Carrot & Parsnip Mash	6
Chicken & Asparagus Lasagne	17
Chicken & Ham Rosti Bake	12
Chicken Balti	14
Coconut Chicken	13
Cooked Breast of Turkey (per Slice)	2
Diced Roast Potatoes	11
Dum Ka Korma	17
French Style Chicken	8
Ham & Pineapple Panini Pizza	10
Lamb Jardaloo	13
Leg of Lamb (per Slice)	4
Mozzarella & Tomato Panini Pizza	7
Nine Jewel Rice	8
Pork Loin with Apricot & Apple Stuffing	8
Potato Dauphinoise	11
Roast Chicken & Stuffing	12
Roasted Vegetable Cous Cous	10
Salmon & Vegetable Pie	12
Sausage & Vegetable Gumbo	26
Topside of Beef (per Slice)	3
Tuscan Vegetables & Chicken Bake	12
Vegetable Lasagne	21

Weight Watchers

Cakes & Sweet Biscuits

Almond Cake Slice	3
Apple Crumble Slices	2
Belgian Chocolate Slices	2
Blueberry & Vanilla Oaty Biscuits	2
Caramel Cake Bars	3
Caramel Mallow Wafers	1
Caramel Shortcakes	3
Caramel Wafers	2
Carrot Cake Slice	2
Chocolate Biscuits	2
Chocolate Mini Roll	2
Country Slice	2
Cranberry & Sunflower Seed Oaty Biscuits	3
Cranberry & Orange Cookies	2
Double Chocolate & Orange Mini Cookies	2
Double Chocolate Chip Cookies	2
Ginger & Lemon Cookies	2
Ginger Crunch Cookies	2
Jaffa Mini Roll	2
Lemon Cake Slice	2
Mini Carrot Cakes	3
Mini Chocolate Cupcakes	2
Mini Flapjack Bites	1
Mini Lemon Cupcakes	1
Mini Victoria Sponges	3
Mixed Seed & Honey Oaty Biscuits	2
Oat Choc Chip Cookies	2
Oat Digestive Biscuits	2
Oaty Chocolate Chip Mini Cookies	2
Raspberry & White Chocolate Cookies	2
Sultana & Cinnamon Cookies	2
Toffee Cookies	2
Wild Blueberry Muffins	5

Quiches

Bacon, Leek & Cheese Quiche	9
Cheese & Onion Crustless Quiche	7
Mediterranean Vegetable Crustless Quiche	6
Quiche Lorraine	8

Sandwiches & Salads

BLT Sandwich	6
Chargrilled Chicken Sandwich	7
Chicken & Bacon Sandwich	7
Chicken Caesar Wrap	8
Chicken Fajita Wrap	8
Egg Mayonnaise & Cress Sandwich	7
Mexican Chicken Pasta Salad	8

Prawn Mayonnaise Sandwich	7
Roast Chicken & Stuffing Sandwich	7
Sweet Chilli Chicken & Ginger Wrap	8
Triple Pack: Prawn, Egg & Chicken Sandwich	10
Tuna & Sweetcorn Pasta Salad	7
Turkey Ham & Coleslaw Sandwich	8

Savoury Biscuits & Snacks

Chargrilled Smokey Bacon Flavour Corn Bites	2
Cheese & Onion Crinkle Crisps	2
Cheese Bites	2
Cheese Curls	2
Cheese Flavour Puffs	2
Hot Chilli Tortillas	2
Mini Hoops, Ready Salted	2
Mini Hoops, Salt & Vinegar Flavour	2
Nacho Cheese Tortillas	2
Ready Salted Crinkle Crisps	2
Roast Chicken Flavour Crinkle Crisps	2
Salt & Black Pepper Tortillas	2
Spicy Mexican Flavour Corn Bites	2
Sun Dried Tomato & Italian Herb Savoury Biscuits	2
Sweet Chilli Flavour Crinkle Crisps	2
Wheat & Oat Crackers	1

Iced Desserts

Caramel Shortcake Luxury Iced Dessert	3
Chocolate & Vanilla Cone	4
Chocolate Brownie Luxury Iced Dessert	3
Chocolate Honeycomb Swirl Minipot	2
Mini Milk Chocolate Stick	2
Mini White Chocolate Stick	3
Mint Chocolate Sundae	3
Raspberry Swirl Minipot	2
Strawberry & Vanilla Cone	4
Strawberry Meringue Luxury Iced Dessert	2
Strawberry Swirl Minipot	2
Toffee Honeycomb Sundae	3
Toffee Swirl Minipot	2

Other Restaurants & Cuisines

Starters & Side Orders

Beef Patties (1 Mini)	8
Breadfruit	3
Callaloo Rice	16
Caribbean Side Salad (No Dressing)	0
Dumpling	8
Gunga Peas	3
Plain Rice (4 tablespoons)	6
Plantain (Fried)	6
Rice & Peas	17
Roti Bread	9
Stew Peas with Spinners	8
Sweet Potato/Yam	4
Sweetcorn	4
Yam, Dumplings & Banana	11

Main Courses

Ackee	4
Ackee & Saltfish	7
Callaloo/Dasheen/Taro	3
Chicken & Sweet Potatoes	10
Chicken Curry with Rice	22
Chicken Pattie	12
Chicken Roti	23
Chicken Rundown	15
Coconut Rundown Vegetables with Rice	14
Curried Goat with Rice	21
Curried Mutton with Rice	18
Escoveltch Fish	15
Jerk Chicken	13
Mutton Pattie	13
Oxtail	19
Saltfish Pattie	12
Sweet Cassava	4
Vegetable Pattie	12

Desserts

Caribbean Fruit Cake with Rum Cream	13
Rum Cake	14
Tropical Crumble with Cream	14

Other Restaurants & Cuisines

West Indian Cuisine

Time to Decide

Meat Antipasti	**16**

Big Plates

Chargrilled Chicken	**13**
Chargrilled Gammon Steak	**26**
Cumberland Sausages	**20**
Goat's Cheese & Sundried Tomato Tart	**18**
Hand Made Organic Salmon & Smoked Haddock Fishcakes	**35**
Lamb Shank	**25**
Mushroom, Onion & Pepper Tart	**16**
Rib Eye Steak	**27**
Sea Bream	**10**
Steak Frites	**23**
Tempura Battered Cod	**31**

Burgers

All Bar One Carb-Free Burger	**10**
Beef & Coriander Burger	**29**
Beef & Coriander Burger with Camembert & Caramelised Onion	**35**
Beef & Coriander Burger with Crispy Prosciutto & Sliced Avocado	**36**
Chicken Fillet Burger	**27**
Chicken Fillet Burger with Bacon & Cheese	**30**
Falafel, Mushroom & Red Pepper Hummus Stack	**34**
Lamb Burger	**30**

Salads & Skewers

Chicken, Bacon & Avocado Salad	**16**
Crispy Duck & Cucumber Salad	**13**
Halloumi with Roasted Vegetables	**11**
Salmon Trout & Oriental Slaw	**11**
Tiger Prawn & Chorizo with Noodles	**16**

Sandwiches

Chargrilled Chicken Sandwich	**19**
Hummus, Lettuce & Sun Dried Tomato Wrap	**13**
Rib Eye Steak Sandwich	**19**
Welsh Rarebit	**15**

Little Dishes

Boxed Baked Camembert	**15**
Calamari	**11**
Chicken & Chorizo Skewers	**9**
Chicken Quesadilla	**12**
Chorizo	**13**
Falafel	**13**
Goat's Cheese Bruschetta	**8**
Hoi Sin Duck Quesadilla	**15**

	ProPoints value
Hummus	14
Meatballs	10
Mini Fishcakes	8
Mushroom Quesadilla	10
Tiger Prawns	5

Bar Nibbles

Fresh Cooked Crisps with Sour Cream & Salsa	9
Marinated Mixed Olives	2
Pistachio Nuts	8
Toasted Ciabatta with Tomato Salsa	6

Sides

Asian Style Noodles	9
Fries	12
House Salad with Balsamic Dressing	2
Oriental Slaw	2
Roasted Vegetables	1
Rustic Parsnip & Sweet Potato Mash	6

Sweet Treats

Banoffee Cheesecake	17
Bite Size Waffles	13
Chocolate Brownie	16
Espresso Ice Cream	5
Melting Chocolate Fondant	21
Treacle Tart	13

Small Dishes

Crispy Duck Spring Rolls	**12**
Crispy Potato Skins	**15**
Homemade Chicken Pâté	**13**
Hot Haddock Smokey	**12**
New England Chowder	**15**
Our BBQ Ribs	**12**
Our Favourite Cajun Mushrooms	**14**
Proper Prawn Cocktail	**12**
Tempura Prawns	**16**
Thai Style Fishcakes	**9**
Wild Mushroom & Balsamic Tart	**11**

Hot off the Grill

21 Day Aged 8oz Sirloin Steak	**26**
21 Day Aged Rib Eye Steak	**36**
Gourmet Burger	**39**
Gourmet Chicken Sandwich	**30**
Surf & Turf 21 Day Aged Sirloin Steak	**34**
Surf & Turf Gourmet Burger	**43**

Slow Cooked Dishes

Braised Beef with Red Wine & Mushrooms	**23**
Our Famous Slow Cooked BBQ Ribs, Classic	**45**
Our Famous Slow Cooked BBQ Ribs, Legendary	**58**
Slow Cooked Shank of Lamb	**26**
Slow Roast Duck Legs	**27**

Freehouse Favourites

Chicken with Smoked Applewood Cheese & Bacon	**22**
Chicken, Ham & Leek Pudding	**32**
Classic Chilli con Carne	**23**
Grilled Halloumi & Cherry Tomato Cassoulet	**16**
Hand-Carved Ham, Eggs & Chips	**22**
Pesto & Parmesan Linguine	**26**
Sausages & Mash	**20**
Southern Indian Prawn Curry	**25**
Warm Bacon & Chicken Salad	**13**
Wild Mushroom & Tarragon Risotto	**16**

Seafood

Homemade Fish & Chips	**31**
Hot Haddock Smokey (Main Course)	**21**
Moules Frites	**18**
Pan Fried Salmon Fillet with Lemon & Caper Butter	**18**
Pan Fried Sea Bass Fillets	**13**
Scampi & Chips	**30**
Smoked Salmon & Spring Onion Fishcake	**22**
Special Recipe Fish Pie	**16**

Sides

Buttery Mash	6
Chips with Bloody Mary Ketchup	12
Creamy Garlic Layer Potatoes	7
Garlic Baguette	13
Garlic Baguette with Cheese	14
Onion Rings	8
Wild Rocket & Parmesan Side Salad	3

Happy Endings

Apple Crumble	14
Banoffee Pie	15
Bread & Butter Pudding	14
Cheese & Biscuits	16
Chocolate Brownie Sundae	29
Créme Brulêe	9
Dairy Ice Cream (per Scoop)	6
Eton Mess	14
Lemon Tart	18
Luxury Belgian Chocolate Waffle	22
Plum Tarte Tatin	13
Sticky Toffee Pudding	26
Sunken Chocolate Pudding	23

Starters

Baked Flat Mushroom	5
Black Pudding, Apple & Chorizo Salad	14
Browns Tiger Prawn Cocktail	12
Chicken & Duck Liver Parfait	9
Crab & Avocado Stack	10
Goat's Cheese & Red Onion Tart	11
Half a Dozen Fresh Oysters	1
Pan Seared Black Pearl Scallops	8
Scottish Langoustine Gratin	14
Slow Roasted Peppers	3

Fish & Salads

Chargrilled Chicken Salad	20
Fish & Chips	26
Monkfish wrapped in Prosciutto	12
Prawn & Chorizo Linguine	17
Roast Pepper, Vine Tomato & Butternut Squash Salad	8
Salmon Fillet	7
Seafood Platter	20
Smoked Fishcakes	15
Whole Baked Sea Bream	12

Main Dishes

28 Day Aged Rib Eye Steak	29
Bacon Cheese Burger	40
Calves Liver & Bacon	17
Chargrilled Fillet Steak	22
Chargrilled Haunch of Venison	14
Chicken Sandwich	30
Chicken Schnitzel	19
Grilled Chicken	31
Grilled Courgette & Mozzarella Tagliolini	23
Guinea Fowl	20
Roast Mediterranean Tart	13
Slowly Braised Pork	19
Slowly Cooked Shoulder of Lamb	21
Steak Frites	20
Steak, Mushroom & Guinness Pie	23

Puddings

Apple Pie with Custard	15
Bread & Butter Pudding	11
Elderflower Jelly	6
Poached Pear	11
Profiteroles	13
Raspberry & Chocolate Brownie	16
Rich Dairy Ice Cream	16
Sticky Toffee Pudding	21

Little Plates

Breaded Jalapeños	8
Chicken Pakora	10
Chicken Piri Piri Split Sticks	7
Chicken Quesadilla	12
Chicken Wings	12
Chilli Nachos	14
Garlic Dough Balls	11
Houmous & Pitta	10
Meat Balls	7
Mushroom & Stilton	12
Nachos	12
Potato Wedges & Bacon	12
Salsa & Chips	9
Sausage Bites with Mustard & Honey	11
Soy Bubble Battered Chicken Strips	12

One Pots

Bacon Carbonara	20
Chicken Tikka Masala	20
Chilli	21
Lasagne	17
Mushroom Carbonara	22
Sausage & Mash	16

Salads

Caesar Salad	7
Chicken Caesar Salad	11
Crayfish Caesar Salad	8
Salmon Caesar Salad	11

Main Dishes

8oz Rump Steak with Fries, Coleslaw & Salad	27
8oz Sirloin Steak with Fries, Coleslaw & Salad	27
Fish & Chips	24
Ribs	43
Roast Chicken	48
Simply Salmon	28
Smoky Mountain Chicken	27

Sandwiches, Wraps & Paninis

Bacon & Cheese Panini	14
Chicken & Bacon Panini	19
Chicken Caesar Wrap	13
Classic Chicken Club Sandwich	13
Classic Crayfish Club Sandwich	11
Mushroom Halloumi Chilli Jam Wrap	10
Peking Duck Wrap	9
Tuna & Cheese Panini	13

Burgers

Cheese & Bacon Burger	39
Chicken Burger	24
Classic Burger	33
Halloumi & Mushroom Burger	26

Chicago's Sizzling Fajitas

Chargrilled Chicken	29
Mushroom & Halloumi	30
Steak	32
Tiger Prawn	28

Jacket Potatoes (No Butter)

Chicken & Bacon	17
Crayfish	16
Mozzarella, Cheddar Cheese & Beans	20
Spicy Beef Chilli	18

Sides

Curly Fries	8
Fries	12
Garlic Bread	9
Garlic Bread with Cheese	15
Onion Rings	8
Side Salad, No Dressing	0
Wedges	10

Desserts

Baileys Ice Cream (per Scoop)	6
Cheesecake	10
Chocolate Fudge Cake	15
Chocolate Pot	7
Ice Cream (3 Scoops)	16
Traditional Apple Pie	13

Filled Croissants

Cheese & Tomato or Ham	13
Chicken Mayonnaise	18
Ham, Cheese & Asparagus	15
Prawn Mayonnaise	14

Paninis & Toasties (with Salad)

Beef & Caramelised Onion Panini	14
Ham & Cheddar Cheese Panini	15
Mozzerella with Sundried Tomatoes & Pesto Panini	14
Mushroom, Bacon & Cheese Panini	14
Sundried Tomato, Cheddar & Mozzerella Cheese Toastie	16
Tuna Melt Panini	16

Sandwiches & Wraps

All Day Breakfast Roll	15
Chicken Caesar Wrap	11
Chicken Mayonnaise Sandwich	12
Egg & Bacon Kaiser Roll	10
Egg Mayonnaise or Tuna Mayonnaise Sandwich	12
Salad Roll with Egg & Cheese	12

Jacket Potatoes (with Salad) & Quiches (with Salad)

Bacon, Mushroom & Cheese or Tuna & Sweetcorn	24
Baked Beans or Coleslaw	19
Broccoli Quiche	10
Cheddar Cheese	21
Cottage Cheese	18
Quiche Lorraine	12

Patisserie

Almond or Butter Croissant	10
Banoffee Éclair	11
Bavarian Apple Flan	7
Black Forest Kirsch	8
Carrot Cake	14
Chocolate Cheesecake or Vanilla Slice	10
Chocolate Éclair	14
Coffee Éclair	15
Fruit Scone	12
Fruit Scone with Jam & Cream	17
Gâteau Noir	19
Lemon Cheesecake or Tarte au Citron	14
Meringue, Fresh Cream	14
Plain Scone or Toasted Teacake & Butter	9
Plain Scone with Jam & Cream	14
Strawberry Tart or Danish Pastry	12

Frankie & Benny's

Other Restaurants & Cuisines

Breads

Bread & Olives	6
Flavoured Garlic Breads – Goat's Cheese & Onion	14
Flavoured Garlic Breads – Mozzarella Cheese	13
Flavoured Garlic Breads – Tomato	10
Flavoured Garlic Breads – Tomato & Pesto	12
Garlic Dough Balls	7
Garlic Pizza Bread	10
Warm Ciabatta Bread	6

Starters

Amazing Skins – BBQ, Chicken, Sweetcorn & Cheddar	16
Amazing Skins – Crispy Bacon, Tomato, Onion & Cheddar	18
Amazing Skins – Goat's Cheese & Home Made Bruschetta	15
Bruschetta	8
Crab Cake	8
Crispy Coated Chicken Strips	11
Frankie's Fried Calamari	11
Mozzarella & Tomato Salad	14
Mushroom Alfredo Crostini	14
Prawn Cocktail	7
Sticky Wings	13
Tiger Prawn Skewer	5

Pasta & Bakes

Cajun Chicken Pasta Bake	23
Chicken & Prawn Alfredo	22
Chicken Carbonara	24
Chicken Penne Arrabbiata	17
Chicken Penne Romana	17
Lasagne al Forno	18
Meatballs on Spaghetti	22
Penne Alfredo	19
Penne Arrabbiata	11
Philly Steak Bake	26
Spaghetti Bolognese	16
Spaghetti Carbonara	21
Spinach & Ricotta Cannelloni	19
Sticky Pasta	18

House Pizzas

American Deli	28
American Hot	22
BBQ Chicken	21
BBQ Meatball	21
Californian	25
Chicken Americano	25
Hawaiian	21
Margherita	18

134

Speciality Pizzas

Boston 7	**39**
Californian Club	**29**
Carbonara	**33**
Louisiana Chicken	**30**
Napoli	**30**

Deep Filled Calzone

Chicago Grinder	**31**
Chicken Carbonara	**30**
Garlic Mushroom & Goat's Cheese	**28**
Meatball Siciliana	**28**
New Yorker	**24**
Siciliana	**24**

House Specialities

BBQ Baby Back Ribs with Fries	**38**
BBQ Chicken & Ribs with Fries	**42**
Beer Battered Cod & Chips	**35**
Benny's Sweet Cured Bacon Steaks with Herb Potatoes	**19**
Frankie's Hotdog	**24**
Mediterranean Vegetable Risotto	**26**
New York Chicken with Fries	**36**
Oven Baked Chicken Parmigana with Jacket Potato	**31**
Salmon Fishcakes with Jacket Potato	**28**
Salt & Pepper Scampi with Fries	**26**
Sausage & Mash	**15**
Sister Rosaria's Lamb Shank with Mashed Potato	**22**

Burgers

Bacon Cheese Burger	**38**
Black & Blue Burger	**42**
Black Pepper Mayo Burger	**35**
Cheeseburger	**35**
Classic Hamburger	**32**
Mediterranean Veg Burger	**24**

Double Stacks

BBQ Double Cheese	**54**
Double Philly Stack	**56**
Manhattan	**56**

Sandwiches

BLT	**28**
Cajun Chicken	**27**
Chicken Caesar	**27**
Chicken Club Triple Decker	**33**
Grilled Chicken Breast	**29**
Frankie's Steak Ciabatta	**32**

Salads

Chicken Breast Caesar	11
Crab	6
Sticky Chicken with Garlic Ciabatta	15
Sticky Prawn with Garlic Ciabatta	12
Warm Chicken with Garlic Ciabatta	12

Desserts

Aunt Carla's Real Dairy Ice Cream	19
Banana Cheesecake	18
Banoffee Sundae	26
Brownies & Ice Cream	23
Cinnamon Waffle Crunch	22
Cookies & Cream Explosion	26
East Coast Sundae	26
Eli's Caramel Pecan Cheesecake	12
Eli's Tiramisu	16
Knickerbocker Glory	16
Mamma's Chocolate Marble	31
Mamma's Crumble with Ice Cream	16
Sorbet	5
Sticky Toffee Pudding	17
Vanilla Cheesecake	12

Sharers & Sides

Cajun Chicken Pieces	11
Chunky GBK Fries, No Dip	12
GBK Corn Chips	11
GBK Homeslaw	2
GBK Salad	9
Grilled Chicken Kebabs	11
Homemade Onion Rings	8
Marinated Mixed Olives	4
Mixed Leaf Salad with House Dressing	2
Rocket & Parmesan Salad	7
Spicy Mixed Nuts	8

Burgers

Avocado & Bacon Beef Burger	27
Avocado, Bacon & Chicken Burger	24
Barbecue Beef Burger	20
Blue Cheese Beef Burger	23
Cajun Beef Burger	20
Camembert, Cranberry & Chicken Burger	22
Cheese Beef Burger	24
Chicken Burger	16
Chilli Beef Burger	22
Classic Beef Burger	20
Garlic Mayo Beef Burger	36
Habanero Beef Burger	23
Kiwiburger	26
Mexican Beef Burger	24
Pesterella Beef Burger	25
Satay Beef Burger	22
Satay Chicken Burger	18
Thai Chicken Burger	16

Vegetarian

Aubergine & Goat's Cheese	16
Falafel	20
Mushroom	22
Puy Lentil	16
Veggie & Camembert	15

Salads

Butternut Squash Salad	8
Chilli Chicken Salad	9
Spiced Bulgar Salad	12
Spiced Bulgar Salad with Grilled Marinated Chicken	14

Breakfast

Brekkie Bap (Egg & Bacon)	25
Daily Oats Organic Porridge	15
Free Range Eggs on Toasted Focaccia	10
Good Morning Brekkie	20
Granola Breakfast Sundae	10
Natural Yogurt & Fresh Fruit	2
Poppy Seed Bagel (with Jam)	10
Smoked Salmon & Free Range Scrambled Eggs	16
Stacked Blueberry & Banana Pancakes	19
Ultimate Superfoods Rude Health Muesli	13

Brunch

Eggs Benedict "Our Way"	17
Full Brunch Plate	32
'Giraffe Favourite' Grilled Chicken Club	19
Grilled Chicken, Bacon & Brie Toasted Baguette	30
Huevos Rancheros Mexican Style Breakfast	21
Huevos Rancheros Mexican Style Breakfast – Vegetarian	13
Toasted Goat's Cheese Focaccia	15
Veggie Brunch Plate	26

Starters

Antipasti Bruschetta Salad	17
Cheesy Garlic Focaccia Skewer	16
Chicken Potstickers	15
Chicken Tikka Sticks	15
Crunchy Japanese Tiger Prawns	5
Edamame	15
Hummus with Warm Naan & Crudites	15
Marinated Olives & Pickles	4

Sharing

Nachos Nirvana (Half)	18
Mezze with Warm Naan (Half)	15
Topped Potato Wedges (Half)	16
Tortilla Chips & House Dips (Half)	10

Burgers

100% English Beef	43
Falafel Deluxe	31
Grilled Cajun Chicken	28
Herby Chicken Schnitzel BLT	37
The Big Greek Lamb Focaccia	27

Sides

Beer Battered Onion Rings	17
Corn on the Cob	4

	ProPoints value
Crispy Potato Wedges	14
Little Caesar Salad	4
Mash	12
Mexican Green Rice Bowl	5
Naan Bread	13
Skin on Fries	10
Steamed Broccoli, Green Beans & Butternut Squash (no Butter)	0

Salads

Chicken, Prawn & Vermicelli Noodle Salad	21
Sunshine Powerfood Salad	16
Super Healthy Veggie & Oregano Feta Salad	20
Sushi Rice Salad with Smoked Salmon	20

Mains

BBQ Baby Back Ribs	34
Good Old Steak & Chips	31
Homemade Beef & Abbot Ale Pie	32
Hot Thai Duck Stir Fry	18
Jambalaya Meatballs on Fettuccine	39
Our Style Pasta 'Primavera'	28
Parmesan Chicken Schnitzel Kiev	20
Peri Peri Grilled Half Chicken (with Chips)	18
Roasted Mushroom, Goat's Cheese & Spinach Flatbread Pizza	28
Wok Fried Vegetables & Udon Noodles Stir Fry	22

Our Mexicana

BBQ Chicken & Smoked Quesadilla	23
Farmers Market Vegetable Burrito	28
Tangy & Spicy Turkey Enchildada	45

Desserts

Apple & Berry Crumble	30
Banana Waffle Split	25
Chocolate Chunk Brownie	28
Milky Bubble Double Chocolate Cheesecake	32
Rocky Road Ice Cream Sundae (Half)	31
Tropical 'Reggae' Sundae	15

Ice Cream

Jude's Dairy Ice Creams, per Scoop	6
Jude's Fresh Fruit Crush Sorbets, per Scoop	2

Starters

Chicken Liver, Pork & Scottish Heather Honey Pâté	13
Chicken Satay Skewers	13
Hot Grilled King Prawns	5
King Prawn Cocktail	13
Lemon & Garlic Chicken Skewers	7
Mushroom Bruschetta	14
Pan-fried Goat's Cheese with Onion Marmalade	14
Smoked Salmon	8
Tomato & Mozzarella	12
Tomato Bruschetta	12

Sharers

Baked Camembert (Half)	12
Nachos (Half)	7
Nachos with Chicken & Peppers (Half)	8

Salads

Chicken & Chorizo	16
Chicken Caesar	15
Greek	15
Tuna Niçoise	14

Fresh from the Grill

7oz British Fillet	21
8oz British Beef Burger	36
8oz British Rump	23
8oz British Sirloin	21
8oz Lincolnshire Pork Loin Steak	23
10oz British Rib-Eye	28
16oz British T-bone	25
Cheese & Bacon 8oz British Beef Burger	43
Chicken Fillet Burger	32
Fresh Grilled Sea Bass	11
Grilled Calves Liver	17
Lemon & Garlic Chicken	13
Mixed Grill	39
Scottish Salmon	12
Welsh Lamb Skewers	18
Yellow Fin Tuna Loin	13

Pasta & Risotto

Butternut Squash, Blue Cheese & Walnut Risotto	24
Chicken & Chorizo Tortiglioni	18
Seafood Risotto	24
Seafood Tagliatelle	21
Stuffed Peppers on Tagliatelle	17

Ha Ha Favourites

10oz Gammon, Eggs & Skinny Chips	28
Chicken Breast with Serrano Ham	17
Fishcakes	26
Hand-Crumbed Haddock Fish Fingers	26
Portobello Mushroom	9
Sausages & Mash	23
Smoked Haddock	19

Side Orders

Braised Red Cabbage with Cranberry & Apple	2
Buttered Carrots	2
Buttered Courgette, Green Beans & Broccoli	2
Coleslaw	6
Garlic Ciabatta	7
Greek Salad	6
Hand-cut Maris Piper Fat Chips with Tartare Sauce	13
Olives	4
Onion Rings	11
Plain Caesar Salad	8
Seasonal Potatoes	5
Skinny Chips with Dijon Mustard Mayonnaise	13

Desserts

Baked Camembert, half	16
Baked Vanilla Cheesecake	14
Brioche Bread & Butter Pudding	15
Chocolate Fondant	20
Crème Brûlée	12
Rich Vanilla Ice Cream	10
Sticky Toffee Pudding	18
Trio of Mini Desserts	14
Warm Chocolate Brownies	13

Baps

Bacon	14
Hot Sausage	17
I Love England	16
Roast Mushroom With Plum Tomatoes	7

Organic Porridge

70% Organic Fairtrade Chocolate	13
Fresh Banana Slices	9
Granola	12
Low GI Organic Blossom Honey	12
Plain	8
Strawberry Compote	10
Toasted Seeds	11

Juices

Carrot & Orange Juice	2
Cloudy Apple with Lime & Mint	3
Fresh Leon-Made Lemonade	3
Fresh Orange Juice	3

Quenchers & Smoothies

Blackcurrant Quenchers	3
Lemon, Ginger & Mint Quenchers	1
Power Smoothie	8
Strawberry Power Smoothie	9

Starters & Sides

Brown Rice	8
Green Sunshine Salad	8
Green Sunshine Salad (without Vinaigrette)	2
Hummus with Bread	15
Hummus without Bread	8
Khobez	7
Leon's Classic Baked Beans	3
Moroccan Meatballs	5
Slaw	4

Hot Dishes

Chilli Chicken	22
Chilli con Carne	20
Grilled Chicken with Aioli	22
Moroccan Meatballs	22
Sweet Potato Falafel with Aioli	20
The Leon Gobi	19

The Leon Wraps

Chicken & Chorizo	13
Chilli Chicken	11
Grilled Chicken	11
Slow-Cooked Shredded Pork	12
Sweet Potato Falafel	12

Superfood Salads

Cajun Crayfish	10
Grilled Chicken with Aioli & Vinagrette	16
Grilled Chicken without Aioli & Vinagrette	11
Originial without Vinaigrette	8
Smoked Mackerel & Beetroot with Aioli & Vinagrette	15
Smoked Mackerel & Beetroot without Aioli & Vinagrette	11
Superfoods Salad – Original with Vinaigrette	14

Daily Seasonal Specials

Leon Rogan Josh	17
Malay Red Curry	20
Moorish Vegetable Tagine	18
Oriental Pork & Beans	18

Soups

Bacon & Chilli Bean	8
Harira (Chickpea with Saffron Veg)	6
Hungarian Beef Goulash	4
Leon Lentil Masala	7
Roast Chicken & Sweetcorn	7
Roy's Tomato	2
Spanish Pork & Beans	5
White Bean & Cheddar	8

Bar Snacks

Chilli Roasted Nuts	15
Olives	3

Puds & Muffins

A Scoop of Organic Vanilla Ice Cream	5
Blueberry Boost Pocket Knickerbocker Glories	9
Brownie & Organic Ice Cream	19
Dark Cherry & Chocolate Pocket Knickerbocker Glories	9
Dark Chocolate Muffin	11
Dark Chocolate Tart	17
Lemon & Ginger Crunch & Organic Ice Cream	16
Mango & Strawberry Pocket Knickerbocker Glories	7
Pecan Pie	17
Pecan, Bran & Maple Muffin	11
White Chocolate & Cranberry Muffin	11

Tea Time & Bits in Between

	ProPoints value
Better Brownie	11
Cranberry & Pecan Flapjack	10
Dark Chocolate Tart	17
Lemon Ginger Crunch	12
Life By Chocolate Mousse	5
Organic Oat & Raisin Cookie	6
Pecan Pie	17
Sweet Sevilla Torta Biscuit	3

Appetisers

Houmous with Peri-Peri Drizzle & Pitta Bread	13
Peri-Peri Nuts	5
Red Pepper Dip	7
Spicy Mixed Olives	6

PERi-PERi Chicken

Chicken Breast, Quarter	8
Chicken, Half	13
Chicken Wings (3)	5
Chicken Wings (5)	8
Chicken Wings (10)	15

Burgers, Pittas & Wraps

Beanie Burger or Pitta	13
Beanie Wrap	19
Chicken Breast Fillet Burger	10
Chicken Breast Fillet Pitta	11
Chicken Breast Fillet Wrap	17
Double Chicken Breast Fillet Burger or Pitta	15
Double Chicken Breast Fillet Wrap	21
Mushroom & Halloumi Cheese Burger or Pitta	10
Portobello Mushroom & Halloumi Cheese Burger or Pitta	9
Portobello Mushroom & Halloumi Cheese Wrap	15
Veggie Burger or Pitta	10
Veggie Wrap	17

Fresh Salads

Caesar	6
Couscous	6
Mediterranean	5

Sides & Extras

Chips – Regular	9
Coleslaw – Regular	9
Corn on the Cob – Regular	5
Creamy Mash – Regular	7
Garlic Bread – Regular	9
Grilled Halloumi Cheese	2
Macho Peas – Regular	5
Nando's Mixed Leaf Salad	1
Perinaise	5
Portuguese Roll	5
Ratatouille	4
Spicy Rice – Regular	5
Sweet Potato Mash	7
Toasted Pitta Bread	5

Aussie-Tizers

Alice Springs Chicken Quesadilla (Regular)	15
Aussie Cheese Fries (Small)	11
Bloomin' Onion	8
Bushman's 'Shrooms	14
Cairns' Calamari	14
Cheesy Garlic Bread	11
Gold Coast Coconut Shrimp	8
Kookaburra Wings	11
Prawn Cocktail	11
Rib & Wing Combo	15
Walkabout Soup of the Day, Baked Potato	22
Walkabout Soup of the Day, Onion	12

Aussie-Tizers To Share

Alice Springs Chicken Quesadilla (Small)	15
Aussie Cheese Fries (Regular)	10
Grilled Shrimp on the Barbie	9

Signature Steaks

New York Strip 8oz	16
Outback Special 6oz	11
Outback Special 8oz	14
Outback Special 12oz	18
Ribeye 9oz	25
The Melbourne 20oz	29
Victoria's Fillet 7oz	16

Outback Favourites

Alice Springs Chicken & Aussie Fries	45
Chicken Adelaide	33
Full Rack Baby Back Ribs & Aussie Fries	64
Griddled Chicken on the Barbie	22
Half Rack, Baby Back Ribs & Aussie Fries	38
Kookaburra Chicken Tenders	33
Long Reach Lamb Chops	50
No Rules Parmesan Pasta	26
No Rules Parmesan Pasta with Chicken	37
No Rules Parmesan Pasta with Chicken & Shrimp	37
No Rules Parmesan Pasta with Shrimp	35
Outback's Famous Ribs on the Barbie	51
Sydney's Smothered Steak	52
Toowoomba Pasta	30

Perfect Combinations

Alice Springs Chicken & Ribs Combination	44
BBQ Chicken & Ribs Platter	44
Outback Grillers – Chicken	20

Outback Grillers – Shrimp	19
Outback Grillers – Salmon	22
Rump & Savoury Shrimp Medley	32

Straight from the Sea

Atlantic Salmon	21
Royal Port Fresh Catch	17
Savoury Shrimp Medley	30

Burgers & Sandwiches

Bacon Cheeseburger	41
BBQ Chicken & Bacon Sandwich	36
No Rules Burger – Burger & Bun with Aussie Fries	20
No Rules Burger with Bacon	25
No Rules Burger with BBQ Sauce	22
No Rules Burger with Blue Cheese Dressing	26
No Rules Burger with Sautéed Mushrooms	23
No Rules Burger with Swiss Cheese	28
The Bloomin' Burger	41
The Outbacker Burger	31
The Ultimate Chicken Melt	39

Desserts

Banoffee Pie	20
Carrot Cake	19
Cheesecake Olivia – no Sauce	10
Cheesecake Olivia – with Chocolate Sauce	24
Cheesecake Olivia – with Raspberry Sauce	15
Chocolate Peanut Butter Pie	37
Chocolate Thunder from Down Under	28
Sweet Adventure Sampler Trio	29
Sydney's Sinful Sundae	28

Appetizers

Boneless Wings	15
Buffalo Wings	17
Garlic Ciabatta Bread, Plain	12
Garlic Ciabatta Bread with Cheese	16
Jack Daniel's Sesame Chicken Strips or Wings for One	14
Loaded Potato Skins	24
Mozzarella Dippers	34
Mushroom Alfredo	16

Appetizers to Share

Cheese Nachos (Half)	20
Chicken Fajita Nachos (Half)	23
Jack Daniel's Tower (Half)	18
Loaded Potato Skins – per serving	12
Times Square Big Share (Quarter)	15

Steaks with Fries

New York Strip	26
Rib-Eye	34
Surf & Turf Combo – Ribeye	36
Surf & Turf Combo – Sirloin	28

Ribs – Full Rack

Friday's BBQ Ribs or Jack Daniel's Ribs	66
Ribs & Shrimp Combo – BBQ Sauce or Jack Daniel's Glaze	61

Jack Daniel's Grill

American Grill	59
Chicken	37
Chicken & Shrimp	44
Salmon	31
Shrimp	42

Prime Choice Burgers

Jack Daniel's Pepperjack	57
Mushroom Swiss	53
Simply Prime Choice	44
Southwest	55

Classic & Loaded Burgers

BBQ Burger	53
Cheesy Bacon Cheeseburger	61
Classic Cheeseburger	44
Classic Hamburger	38
Friday's Burger – Bacon Cheeseburger	48
Jack Daniel's Monterey Burger	57

Double Stacked

Burger	**64**
Cheeseburger	**70**
Friday's Burger – Bacon Cheeseburger	**77**
Jack Daniel's Monterey Burger	**78**

Chicken

Chicken Fingers	**36**
Sizzling Chicken	**38**
Wicked Chicken	**33**

Sandwiches with Fries

Cajun Chicken Ciabatta	**37**
Chicken Finger BLT	**42**
Grilled Chicken Sandwich	**30**
San Fran Sandwich	**36**

Southwest

Cajun-Spiced Chicken Quesadilla	**36**
Cajun-Spiced Vegetable Quesadilla	**30**
Sizzling Fajita with Chicken	**29**
Sizzling Fajita with Chicken & Steak	**38**
Sizzling Fajita with Steak	**34**
Sizzling Vegetable Fajita	**25**

Pasta

Cajun Cream Chicken Penne	**30**
Chicken Alfredo	**36**
Spicy Diablo Pasta	**18**

Salads

BBQ Chicken Salad	**21**
Chicken Caesar Salad	**24**
Jack Daniel's Salmon Salad	**20**
Jack Daniel's Shrimp Salad	**17**

Side Orders

Cajun Onion Rings	**19**
Garlic Ciabatta Bread	**12**
Garlic Ciabatta Bread with Cheese	**16**
Jack Daniel's Special Shrimp	**22**
Mozzarella Dippers	**34**

Desserts

Apple Crunch Waffle	**25**
Chocolate Fudge Fixation	**33**
Cinnamon Swirl Cheesecake	**29**
Dirt Cake	**35**

Cold Meze

Dolmades	7
Fakés Salata	12
Gigandes Plaki	4
Greek Flatbread	19
Htipiti	8
Hummus	7
Kolisalata	27
Melitzanosalata	6
Octopodi Zaffrani	3
Revithia	8
Santorinian Fava or Skordalia	6
Skordalia	6
Tabouleh	13
Taramasalata	16
Taratori	3
Tzatziki	4

Hot Meze

Anatolian Spices Gambas	8
Bifteki with Yoghurt	7
Chicken Skewer	3
Crevettes Saganaki	9
Grilled Asparagus	4
Grilled Halloumi	6
Grilled Kalamari	5
Grilled Octopus or Grilled Sardines	9
Halloumi Melitzano	2
Halloumi Skewer	6
Lamb Cutlets	10
Lamb Kefte	8
Lamb Skewer	7
Pork Skewer	10
Saganaki Kefalotyri	11
Salt Cod	9
Tiropitakia	11
Whitebait (Half)	17

Souvlaki

Chicken	11
Halloumi & Vegetable	15
Lamb	16
Pork	13
Soutzouki	23

Salads & Sides

Cretan Salad	3
Greek Salad	19
Horta Salad	11
Saffron Rice	11

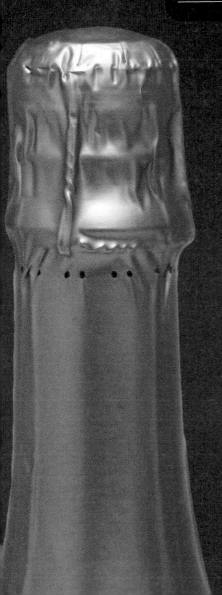

Drinking Out

Alcohol is high in *ProPoints* values and if you are watching what you eat, the last thing you want is for your tipple to topple your weight loss. Excess alcohol is a common culprit behind abdominal fat (it's not called a beer belly for nothing) and alcohol can weaken the strongest resolve and make high-fat snacks look more appealing. We're not suggesting you become a hermit – moderation is the key. So here are some top tips…

Know your units – the recommended guidelines for drinking are no more than: **women**: 2-3 units per day; **men**: 2-4 units per day.

How strong is your drink – the range and strength of alcoholic drinks is on the up and it can be hard to work out just how many units you are drinking. Just one pint of strong lager can equate to more than three units of alcohol and a standard glass of robust New World wine can weigh in at 2½ units. Find out more at www. drinkaware.co.uk.

Large or small – a standard glass of wine used to be 125ml (around one unit of alcohol) but many pubs now offer a range of sizes including a 'small' 175ml glass and a 'large' 250ml glass – that's about a third of a bottle. Spirits used to come in 25ml measures but many pubs or bars now serve them in 35ml or 50ml measures.

Strategies to lower your alcohol *ProPoints* values

- Drink spritzers if you like wine and shandy if you're a beer drinker – you get a long drink but it contains less alcohol.

- Alternate alcoholic drinks with sugar-free soft drinks.

- Make sure there's water on the table (ask the waiter for tap water – it's free and environmentally friendly).

- Offer to drive – you'll be popular and you'll save on 'empty' *ProPoints* values.

- Ask the waiter not to keep filling your glass – it makes you more likely to drink more and it makes it harder to monitor your consumption.

Alcopops – per bottle

Bacardi Breezer, All Flavours	4
Bacardi Breezer, Half Sugar, Raspberry	1
VK LO, Pineapple & Grapefruit	1

Beer, Cider & Lager – per ½ pint unless stated

Beer, Bitter or Light Ale	3
Bottled Beer, Bitter or Lager, 1 bottle (330ml)	4
Cider, Dry	4
Cider, Low Alcohol	2
Coors Light	4
Guinness Original	3
Lager	3
Lager, Light or Low Alcohol, 1 bottle (330ml)	1
Lager, Alcohol Free	1
Magners Light Irish Cider (250ml)	3
Sainsbury's German Lager, Low Alcohol (330ml)	3

Spirits & Liqueurs – per 25ml unless stated

Advocaat	2
Brandy	2
Gin	2
Liqueur, High Strength	3
Liqueur, Medium Strength	2
Pimms	2
Rum	2
Schnapps, Fruit Flavour	3
Tequilla	2
Vermouth, Dry (50ml)	2
Vermouth, Sweet (50ml)	3
Vodka	2
Whiskey/Bourbon	2

Wine & Champagne – per 175ml unless stated

Champagne	5
Port (50ml)	3
Sherry, Dry, Medium or Sweet (50ml)	2
White, Dry	4
White, Medium	5
White, Sweet	6
Red	4
Rosé	4

Soft Drinks – per 250ml unless stated

Bitter Lemon	2
Cola, can (330ml)	4
Ginger Beer, can (330ml)	5
Lemonade, can (330ml)	2
Orange or Pineapple Juice	3

Index